Successful Winemaking At Home

Also by H. E. Bravery
Home Brewing Without Failures (Arc)

H. E. BRAVERY

Successful Winemaking At Home

AN
ARC
BOOK
ARCO PUBLISHING COMPANY, INC.
219 Park Avenue South, New York, N.Y. 10003

An ARC Book
Published by ARCO PUBLISHING COMPANY, INC.
219 Park Avenue South, New York, N.Y. 10003

Revised Edition
Eighth Printing, 1972

Library of Congress Catalog Card Number 62-12119
ISBN 0-668-00861-X

Printed in the United States of America

Preface

NEVER before in the long, long history of home wine-making has the hobby enjoyed such tremendous popularity as it does today, with thousands of new enthusiasts joining our ranks every week. Fortunately we no longer have to follow antiquated methods and recipes that so often resulted in cloudy wines that would not clear, sour wines, acid wines or wines that turned into vinegar. Nor are we bothered with massive tubs and giant jars and masses of bottles of fermenting wines corked loosely (one of the main causes of spoiled wines) or any of the paraphernalia of the home wine-maker of a few short years ago. Modern methods are quick, clean, simple and sure. The result is perfect wines high in alcohol with that brilliance of clarity users of older methods will not believe until seeing for themselves.

The recipes contained in this book have been evolved by varying methods of mine which have appeared elsewhere in many magazines and which, following more than twenty years of experimenting in wine-making have proved to be the best, not only for making all the well-known home wines but for making genuine Vermouth, both French and Italian, and wines savouring of all the world-famous liqueurs including cherry brandy, Kirsch, Kümmel, Curaçao, Morasquin and many others. The lemon gin wine recipe and orange gin wine recipe are the results of my most recent experiments and I take pride in offering them to my readers all over the world. As with all home wines, none of these specialities requires added spirit.

I must record my sincere thanks to the commercial firms

who have so kindly supplied me with a variety of ingredients for my experiments, in particular to Semplex, of Old Hall Works, Stuart Road, Higher Tranmere, Birkenhead, and to H. J. Ruzicka ('Fermenta'), of 95 Frampton Street, London, N.W.8, to R. H. and Meryl Stoner, and to the chief chemist and manager of a famous British winery (who wish to remain anonymous), for guidance during my early years of winemaking.

H. E. BRAVERY

Contents

About The Author

H.E. BRAVERY has been making wines for over twenty years but took to writing about the subject comparatively recently. He has contributed many articles on home wine-making to the *Smallholder, Do It Yourself,* and the *Gardener's Chronicle,* as well as to other journals, and he also lectures on the subject.

The making of wine has been the author's life study, and he has examined the scientific and chemical aspects as well as the theoretical and practical side of the art. He is well known throughout Europe and has a large international following. Mr. Bravery's recipes are famous wherever wine is made, and in this book he passes on the results of his most recent successful experiments in achieving trouble-free, top-quality, full-bodied wines.

Mr. Bravery is also the author of a brand new book, *Home Brewing Without Failures* (Arc, 95 cents), in which he shows how you can make your own beer (light and dark), ale, mead, stout, and cider. Every detail of home brewing is covered step by step in Mr. Bravery's customary thorough, clear, easy-to-follow style, and he includes numerous recipes for making delicious brews.

In 1964, enthusiasts in this country formed the Bravery Wine Club of America. For further information on this club, write to Bravery Wine Club of America, c/o Dr. A. R. Rustebakke, Placitas, Sandoval County, New Mexico.

Introduction

A chat about winemaking

WHEN you have read the various directions in other parts of this book it will be clear that we must approach the making of wine, not with the seriousness that becomes almost painful, but in a similar manner to the way one would set about making good jam or a decent cake. No one would mix the necessary ingredients for these in a fire bucket and put them into a rusty tin or dirty jar and try to cook them over a candle. Yet this is the kind of thing many people do when making wines; but only because they have been led for many years to believe that making wines was simply a matter of knocking together a mixture of ingredients, and then fermenting them under any existing unhygienic conditions. This sort of thing gave many people the impression that home-made wines weren't worth bothering with because, while they made a stop-gap drink, they weren't really very nice. This has been the cause of home-made wines getting a bad name and making thousands of people give up the hobby before they could realize that home-made wines *can* really be magnificent if made in the right way. I could list hundreds of distinguished men and women who make their own wines—retired services commanders, doctors, and people such as Conrad Phillips of William Tell fame who makes his own wine, but I wish to convey my methods to everyone. It is no idle boast to claim that by following my directions your wines will be better than any you have made before. This is because all my methods and recipes are tried and proved and experience shows how spoilage can easily be prevented by the simple

7

rules which ensure success. It all boils down to this: use a good yeast and nutrient, sterilize everything used, keep fermenting brews warm, and keep them covered at all stages of production—all part of a simple routine. You will make very good wines with bakers' yeast and a nutrient, provided you keep the 'must' warm during fermentation, but by using wine yeast your wines will be vastly improved. Wine yeast settles to a sediment like cheese-paste leaving a brilliant wine above it, instead of, as bakers' yeast often does, leaving a cloud in the wine that can only be removed with isinglass or some other clarifying medium.

It is important to understand that a recipe is merely a list of ingredients in varied proportions that will make a wine suit different palates. Anyone can invent a recipe, but it does not follow that everybody can invent a good one. There are too many factors to be considered for that, the main one being that the acid and sugar content of fruit varies from season to season. Even the same variety of fruit grown on the same tree in the same garden will not be identical in two consecutive seasons. Nor will the fruit be the same when grown in the same season if in different gardens because the soil, situation, the amount of sun or shade all affect the acid and sugar content. However, this need not bother you if you follow the recipes. Even here you need not adhere to one too faithfully. A half-pound too little of the fruit will not matter, but a half-pound too much would, because you would be putting in more acid and tannin. Neither will it matter if you do not have quite enough fruit to start with because this may be added any time during fermentation. From the large number of letters I receive it is clear that too many beginners—and not beginners only—are nervous of using their common sense. They think up all sorts of good, solid common-sense ideas and then write asking if, in my opinion, they are good ideas after all.

Provided the simple rules which ensure success are observed, you can do almost anything you like; mix ingredients to get special results, use more yeast if you want to, start half-gallon lots of one kind of wine and then mix them before fermentation has ceased—in fact, do almost anything except use more of the main ingredient listed in whichever recipe you happen to be using.

Do not make a wine just because some particular fruit has become available; think first. If you are not fond of a particular fruit the chances are that you will not like wine made from it.

When you bottle, bottle only perfectly clear wine and don't use any old bottle which happens to be available. It is worth while taking the trouble to use wine bottles all the time; dark ones for red wines, clear glass for lighter wines— and they should be the sort that have an indenture or 'punt' at the bottom. A punt is the part of the bottle which has been pushed up inside. Use decent labels, even if they are plain ones, rather than strips of gummed paper of any shape or size.

The absolute beginner cannot be expected to appreciate that after few attempts the resulting wines will be so good that only the best bottle and label and seal will be suitable for them. I am perfectly serious—I wouldn't dream of putting my wines in any but the best bottles.

I want everyone whoever they may be to realize that they can make wines fit for a king by putting their minds to it.

Beginners often mistakenly imagine that a wine yeast will flavour wines of port or sherry or of whichever yeast is used. This is not so. The name the yeast carries is usually the name of the area from which it comes—but not always.

It is best to use, as we shall see later on, the most suitable variety of yeast for the kind of fruit being used, or for the type of wine being made from that fruit, e.g. it is best to use a port yeast with fruits that ordinarily make a port-style wine, or a burgundy yeast if you are making that type of wine—even though the fruit being used is also made into port-style wines. The different wine types are possible from one variety of fruit merely by altering the amount of fruit and sugar, but all this is fully covered later on. Although I advise wine yeast in all but the root wines and dried fruit wine recipes, I imagine that most of you will settle for bakers' yeast—at least in the early stages of your wine-making and then, as you progress, you will realize that if such wonderful wines can be made with bakers' yeast and household sugar, then surely even better wine would result from using wine yeast and invert sugar. So progress goes on, our wines improving with our experience and as we are able to think for ourselves we find we no longer have to follow too closely a set of hard and fast rules and do better by using our imagination than we ever thought possible.

IMPORTANT NOTE:
Federal regulations and Internal Revenue law provide that the head of any family may, without payment of tax, produce not more than 200 gallons of wine per year for the use of his family, and not for sale, if he registers to do so. He must obtain Form 1541 from the U.S. Treasury Department, Internal Revenue Service, fill out this form, and send it to the Assistant Regional Commissioner of the region in which he resides. No payment of tax is required.

Anyone who intends to produce more than 200 gallons of wine per year, or who intends to produce wine for sale, must obtain a special permit from the Assistant Regional Commissioner (Alcohol and Tobacco Tax), file bond, and meet other requirements for the operation of a bonded wine cellar.

Successful Winemaking At Home

CHAPTER ONE

Essential information

THE simple methods described here are designed for beginners who do not know where to begin and for those with some experience who frequently run into difficulties and disappointments.

The making of top-quality wines is absurdly simple, yet not quite so simple that we can be careless about it. Too many people are still following granny's methods—fermenting in uncovered vessels, allowing fruit mixtures to ferment of their own accord, leaving bottles of fermenting wines corked loosely (the three main causes of ruined wines), while others are still preparing their fruits and other ingredients in a manner which nine times out of ten produces cloudy, acid wines that more often than not find their way down the drain. If readers' previous attempts have not been up to expectations there is a reason. This will be found within these pages as well as the essential, yet simple, information that ensures success in making what is, surely, the finest home product on earth.

In my lectures and in my wine articles which appear in magazines, I repeatedly make it clear that I am an advocate of simplicity. There are many highly complicated scientific and chemical aspects underlying amateur wine-making. A few home operators begin to dabble in these, so that, to them, wine-making becomes a gruelling test of knowledge and skill. Expensive laboratory equipment becomes necessary as does some experience in laboratory techniques and from then on all pleasures are lost in a worrying maze of technicalities. And all for no reason at all, because their wines are no better than those turned out by the simple methods and recipes here. However, so that readers understand the reasons for wines being spoiled, I have included a few chemical details so that the veriest beginner not only knows what to do and how to do it, but also why he is doing it in one particular way. Success is thus assured. Nevertheless, he will need no knowledge of chemistry and no more in the way of utensils than is already available in most homes.

Utensils

For making wines with the recipes and ingredients here all one needs is a gallon-size glass bottle, an unchipped enamel saucepan and a polythene pail. Make certain to use polythene as some plastics are not suitable. Do not use aluminium or copper vessels and do not use an enamel vessel not ordinarily intended for cooking purposes as these often contain lead in the glaze, and this could render wines poisonous.

Gallon-size glass bottles may be had from most chemists or wholesale grocers for about $.25. Fermentation will not be carried out in an open vessel such as a crock or polythene pail in all these recipes unless you want it to; it is best to ferment the liquors in the gallon-size glass bottle—this point will be covered again later on. A polythene pail is necessary for only a few of the recipes and may be disregarded for the time being.

Fermentation

This is the process by which the liquors we prepare are turned into wine, and we have nothing to do with it. All we do when making wine is to prepare a liquid containing substances that will give a pleasant flavour to what will eventually become a finished wine. The yeast we add turns the liquid into wine for us.

Ordinarily, bakers' yeast and white granulated sugar are used by the average home wine maker. However, over the past few years wine-making has taken such a hold that suppliers of equipment and ingredients offer a wide range of yeasts specially imported from the wine-producing areas of France, Italy and Germany. These yeasts make the finest wines because they are true wine yeasts whereas bakers' yeast is only bread yeast and should not be expected to make good wine—though of course it does, but not to be compared with the results following the use of wine yeasts.

Wine yeast is capable of producing eighteen per cent of alcohol by volume (32° proof), against the fourteen per cent of bakers' yeast.

More and more people are using these wine yeasts together with invert sugar instead of household sugar.

Now let us understand what happens when we add yeast to a prepared liquor containing sugar.

Yeast is obtainable in the form of a compressed cake, dried tablet, pellet or in powder form and as a liquid culture, and all are inactive (dormant) at the time of purchase.

Yeast is a living thing—a plant or fungus, it has not been decided which—and when introduced into a sugar solution such as those we shall be preparing it begins almost at once to reproduce itself. Billions of living cells so tiny that three thousand could comfortably queue across a halfpenny begin their life cycle and in doing so produce alcohol and carbon dioxide gas. As will be appreciated, the alcohol we seek is merely a by-product of yeast reproduction.

Many, many generations of yeast are 'born', grow up and die in the course of turning a prepared liquor into wine. So rapid is this reproduction that within hours of the yeast being added to beerwort in the brewery, a knobbly eider-down of new yeast four feet thick covers the whole fermentation tank. Most of this is taken off and pressed for sale or cold-stored for future use.

When making our wines fermentation is seen as a slight frothing during the early stages and this soon settles down to a gentle ferment that may last as long as six months. But if warmth is given—as we shall see later on—fermentation should be over and done with in half that time.

All the time fermentation is going on; that is, all the time the yeast continues to reproduce itself, the amount of alcohol in the wine increases. But it cannot go on for ever because when what we call the maximum alcohol tolerance of the yeast is reached, the alcohol formed kills the yeast. It will be seen then that from the tiny amount of yeast we add at the start masses of new yeast is made and all this helps to make alcohol until the last surviving generation of the original yeast is finally destroyed by the alcohol it and all the other generations put together have formed since we began. When this happens, fermentation ceases and no more alcohol is made. Thus the old tale that the longer wine is kept the stronger it becomes is proved a fallacy—or old wives' tale.

As already mentioned, bakers' yeast can make up to fourteen per cent of alcohol by volume, while wine yeast makes from fifteen per cent to eighteen per cent by volume.

To get the maximum alcohol and to get fermentation over without undue waste of time we must keep the fermenting wine warm. The ideal temperature at which to keep a 'must' is between 65° F. and 70° F. However, few can manage this, but if fermenting wines are kept warm throughout fermentation time, this will do. Most people use an airing cupboard for this and it works well. Others use all sorts of ingenious devices and these are described under the heading 'Aids to Fermentation'. Do not be tempted to keep a 'must' *hot* during fermentation; during the warmer weather almost any warm spot in the kitchen will do, but during cold weather and especially during very cold nights it is always best if a little added warmth can be given.

When a ferment is allowed to become cold the yeast ceases to work. This means that at some time later, if the weather turns warm, fermentation begins again. If the wine has been bottled in the belief that fermentation has ceased for good, the result is a popping under the stairs and corks flying in all directions and the loss of valuable wine.

Aids to Fermentation

Most beginners will be content to keep their fermenting wines warm in an airing cupboard or near the boiler in the kitchen. Others will want to know how they can make a special fermenting cupboard.

If only two or three jars of wine are fermenting at one time, a small cupboard with a small electric heater installed will be ideal. Alternatively, an electric light bulb hanging in a cupboard and the jars grouped round this will serve the purpose just as well, especially if the cupboard is just large enough to accommodate the jars and not so big that a lot of warmth is lost. I know of people who group several jars round a small safety paraffin lamp, but this would only be satisfactory when the wine is under a fermentation lock otherwise the wine might become tainted by fumes. See 'Fermentation Locks', page 22.

Other aids to satisfactory fermentation are good nutrients. Yeast nutrients, as they are called, are carefully balanced yeast foods which assist the yeast to reproduce and therefore make the largest possible amount of alcohol. Sufficient nutrient speeds fermentation so much that, once you have used a good one, you will always do so. I know from my vast experience that warmth, a good yeast and good nutrient will together make wines ten times better than any old yeast, no nutrient and a warm atmosphere one day and a chilly one the next. We want the best; very well, let us take just that little extra care and spend those few extra coppers which will make such an immense difference to the finished product.

Suppliers of special ingredients (see list at the end of this book) offer a variety of nutrients all accompanied by directions how to prepare. In most cases it is just a matter of mixing the nutrient with some of the prepared liquor and then adding it to the brew with the yeast.

Now, a word about 'invert' sugar. Most of you will be content to use household sugar and it is household sugar that I include in the recipes. However, I have proved beyond doubt that invert sugar gives better results. This is also obtainable from the same firms at about 20 cents a pound.

A summary of the foregoing is this: the inexperienced wine maker who uses bakers' yeast, no nutrient, household sugar and who allows the wine to ferment anywhere cannot possibly expect the results which can be achieved by following my advice. By doing so anyone, including beginners who do not have to endure years of apprenticeship, with the aid of a fermentation lock, see page 22, by keeping the wine warm during the whole of the fermenting period, using the appropriate wine yeast, invert sugar and nutrient will obtain wines with a strength, clarity, flavour and bouquet of which they will be justly proud.

When bakers' yeast is used it is crumbled into the prepared

liquor. When wine yeast is used the directions supplied by the dealer must be followed. This involves starting what is called a 'nucleus ferment'. A half-pint milk bottle will do for this. About a quarter-pint of water and a teaspoonful of sugar are boiled together for a minute and then allowed to cool. This is then put into the milk bottle—sterilized as directed later on—and the yeast then added in whatever form it is obtained.

The neck of the bottle is then plugged with cotton wool and put into a warm place. Within a few days—usually three—this little lot is fermenting merrily ready for adding to a batch of wine that you will be waiting to make.

If you prepare the liquor for wine-making and then add the wine yeast it will take three or four days to begin to ferment. Better therefore to get the nucleus fermenting ready to add to the liquor when you have prepared it so that the whole lot is quickly in a state of vigorous fermentation.

It is most important that the yeast is not added to hot water and that the nucleus is not added to hot wine because a temperature well below boiling will destroy the yeast. Let the little drop of sugar-water cool well before adding the yeast and later let the prepared liquor cool well before adding the nucleus or 'starter bottle' as we call it. In the recipes I shall refer to adding the yeast as 'adding the nucleus' on the assumption that you will have taken my advice and will be using wine yeasts prepared as directed, but if you must use bakers' yeast merely crumble this into the liquor at the time you would add the nucleus.

It will be seen in the recipes that all the sugar is not used at once, this is because yeast ferments much better if the sugar is fed to it in stages. Too much sugar at the outset might cause the yeast to stop fermenting at around ten per cent of alcohol. Inexperienced operators might think fermentation has finished naturally and put their wine in a cool place to clear—which, of course it would do. But it would be an over-sweet wine likely to start fermenting again at any time.

For a simple re-statement; having prepared the liquor as the recipes advise, the yeast or nucleus is added together with the nutrient and the wine put in a warm place until all fermentation has ceased.

In some of the recipes (chiefly those calling for flavouring to be added at a late stage of production), directions read: 'leave until fermentation has nearly ceased'. This is rather a broad term for beginners, but where fermentation locks are in use they will know when this stage is reached because the water will remain pushed up to one side of the lock and a bubble just manages to push through every two of three minutes.

Where fermentation locks are not in use, but where clear-glass jars are being used, beginners will be able to see the bubbles of gas rising. All the time there is quite a mass of them rising steadily, fermentation is quite vigorous. But when there is only the faintest trace of a line of bubbles round the perimeter of the wine and where only a few bubbles are seen rising slowly to the surface they may say, for all intents and purposes, that fermentation has nearly ceased—though it may go on for several more weeks.

The Clearing Process

With the recipes and methods described here there is no need to use isinglass or any other aids to clarifying. These wines clear themselves usually before fermentation has ceased. Indeed, it is usual to have a brilliantly clear wine a month before fermentation has ceased. If one or two lots of wine appear to be slow to clear, do not worry, a week or two after fermentation has finally stopped clarifying will take place very quickly. It is important to bear in mind that a clear wine usually has a little deposit to throw, so that it is always best to leave the wine for at least a month after it has become crystal clear in order that the last of the impurities and perhaps some unseen yeast cloud has time to settle out. If this is not done, a slight sediment might form in the bottles and when you begin to pour the wine into a glass the sediment is churned up so that it clouds the wine. Such a happening is not a calamity as the cloud will settle again, probably overnight, but it means putting the bottle away.

It is best when all fermentation has ceased, to siphon the clear wine (if it is not yet crystal clear) into another jar leaving the deposit behind. Then when the wine is finally crystal clear it should be siphoned into bottles. This racking, as we call it, helps to get the slight cloudiness to settle out quickly. See 'Siphoning and Bottling', page 27.

The Enemies

The enemies of successful wine-making are wild yeasts and acetic bacteria. The acetic bacteria which converts alcohol into acetic acid thereby turning wine to vinegar is ever present in the air.

Similarly, the yeasts and spores of fungi which turn wine insipid and flat or turn it sour are also in the air. When using fresh fruit and other ingredients from the garden or from shops these bacteria and yeasts and fungi are already on them, but they are easily destroyed so that they do no harm. The ingredients we shall be using will be supplied in sealed containers so that they will not already be contaminated by the causes of spoilage—as we call them.

However, the water we use might contain harmful bacteria

that can spoil the wine or possibly wild yeast which can cause what we call 'undesirable' ferments. These ferments give 'off' flavours to put it politely—otherwise sour flavours as we refer to sourness in milk—not acid flavours.

Anyway, the methods described here ensure the destruction of all harmful yeasts and bacteria at the outset so they need not worry you.

Now, if wild yeasts and bacteria are in the air they must be on corks, inside bottles and jars; indeed, they are on everything we use. But they are easily destroyed so that success is assured.

It is not generally known that the moulds on cheese, half-empty pots of meat paste and jam are often yeasts growing there, and it is this kind of yeast floating about in the air that ruins our wines if we allow it to settle. To defeat this souring yeast we must keep our fermenting wines and finished wines covered closely. Treatment of finished wines is covered under the heading 'storing'. Covering fermenting wines in jars is very simple, but most important.

As soon as the prepared yeast has been added to the prepared liquid the top of the jar should be covered with a piece of polythene. This should be pressed down all round by hand and strong thin string tied tightly round. This will keep airborne diseases away from the wine because the gas generated during fermentation will find an outlet for itself and keep up a constant outgoing stream, thus preventing the diseases air contains from gaining access. Far better than this polythene covering is a *fermentation lock*.

There are many types available, but the design I like best is the one illustrated in Figure 1.

The whole idea of fitting a fermentation lock is to prevent air and airborne diseases reaching the wine. Firstly, the lock is fitted to a drilled cork and the cork then fitted to the jar—see Figure 2A. Water is then poured into the level shown. The gas formed during fermentation pushes through the water in the form of bubbles, but air-borne diseases are kept out. Better than water in the lock is a little of the sterilizing solution given on page 26, or a crushed and dissolved Campden tablet. This is best because if as sometimes happens a vacuum forms in the jar the air drawn in is purified by the sterilizing solution. When a vacuum forms inside the jar the lock works in reverse for a

Figure. 1. A good type of fermentation lock showing the drilled cork or bung fitted in position. Note that the long end goes through the bung.

while and this often happens when warm wine is put into a
jar and the lock fitted at once. But don't worry if this
happens, because as soon as gas has been generated the
lock will begin working properly.

Another advantage of having a fermentation lock in use
is that it indicates when fermentation has ceased.

All the time bubbles are passing through, and all the
time the water in the lock remains pushed up to one side, it
means that there is pressure in the jar and that this pressure
is gas being formed by the act of fermentation. When
fermentation ceases for good, the water returns to normal.
During the early stages of fermentation, bubbles are run-
ning through the water at the rate of one a second or even
faster than this. But as fermentation slows down they become far less frequent. Later on, the water remains pushed
up to one side and it may take five or even ten minutes for
sufficient gas to form to make one bubble. During the very
last stages of fermentation, it may take a week for one
bubble to push through. Clearly, then, all the time the water
remains pushed up to one side the wine should be left, as it
is safe to say that fermentation is still going on.

When the water returns to normal, give the jar a vigorous
twist and the chances are that you will get fermentation on
the go again for a day or two longer. If the whole idea in
using locks is to keep airborne diseases from contaminating
the wine we must ensure that the bung and the lock are
airtight. If they are not, the gas will escape and no matter
how vigorous fermentation might be, the water in the lock
will remain level. The gas leaking will prevent air reaching
the wine during the early stages, but as it slows down the
outgoing stream of gas through the leakage holes would
not be strong enough for this so that airborne diseases
could easily reach the wine.

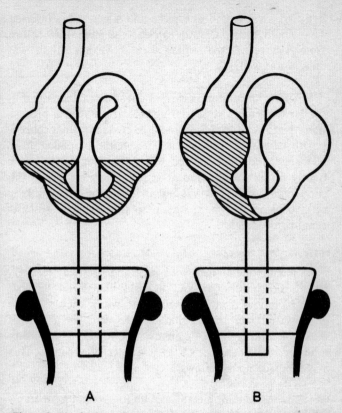

Figure 2. The fermentation lock fitted to the jar. A. Water is poured in to level shown. B. Position of water immediately before a gas bubble passes through.

Having fitted the lock to the bung and jar as shown above, run a little sealing wax round where the bungs enter the jar and where the lock enters the bung. This precaution may not be necessary, but it is better to be on the safe side. When fermentation has ceased the lock and bung are removed in one piece and a new bung inserted. The wine is then put away to clear—as mentioned before. **Note.** I have advised sealing wax above but candle wax does just as well.

Where fermentation is carried on in a polythene pail or similar fermenting vessel during the early stages of production, the top of the vessel should be covered with a sheet of polythene with no holes in it. This should be pulled down all round and then secured with thin strong string or a tightly fitting elastic band. The gas generated during this early vigorous ferment will find an outlet for itself and keep up a constant outgoing stream so that airborne diseases cannot gain access.

Sterilization

As already mentioned, wild yeast and bacteria are likely to be inside bottles, jars and on corks, etc. Therefore, if we are to prevent them damaging our wines they must be destroyed. Better than boiling bottles, etc., in a pail of water or baking them in an oven is to use a sterilizing solution that does the job in a matter of seconds. This may be made up as follows:

Get 2 oz. of sodium metabisulphite (or potassium metabisulphite), there being two forms, from any chemist for about $.20. Nearly fill a half-gallon bottle with warm water and then add the crystals (or powder) and revolve the jar until all is dissolved. Try to use a glass-stoppered jar or bottle from a chemist for this—they'll usually let you have one for about $.20.

To sterilize bottles and jars with this, pour a pint into the first bottle and shake it up so that all the inside is wetted. Then pour it into the next bottle and so on and then back to the bulk again. Having treated the bottles, it is best to rinse them out with boiled water that has cooled well. This will rid the bottles of the rather pungent odour of the sterilizing solution. But don't worry if a slight whiff remains in the bottles, because it will do no harm. Having rinsed the bottles, let them drain for a minute or two and they are now ready for use.

Corks. More wine has been ruined through using un-sterilized corks than through any other cause. The crevices of corks teem with all sorts of harmful bacteria and spoilage yeasts. The best way to sterilize them is to put them in a small basin with something heavy on top to keep them submerged—a heavy cup will do—and then cover with the sterilizing solution. Leave this for about ten minutes and during the time you are bottling a batch of wine. As each cork is required, take it, dip it in boiled water and then wipe it dry with a cloth dipped in the sterilizing solution—which, incidentally, is known as sulphur dioxide or sulphite solution.

The drying of corks is necessary to prevent the weight of the wine pushing out the corks when the bottles are put away on their sides.

Siphoning, Bottling and Storing

It is almost impossible to pour clear wine from one bottle to another without stirring up the lees (deposit). The best method is to siphon the clear wine at bottling time.

First, put the bottle or jar of wine on a table and the empty bottles on a box or stool on the floor. Then, using a yard and a half of surgical rubber or plastic tubing, siphoning is quite a simple operation. Put one end of the tubing in the full jar (or the first of the full bottles) and suck the other end until the wine comes. As soon as this happens, pinch the tube at your lips and, while holding on tightly, put this end in the first empty bottle and let the wine flow. As the empty bottle nearly fills, slowly press the tube between finger and thumb in order to cut off the flow slowly rather than with a jerk. Sudden stoppage often stirs up the deposit. When the bottle has filled to the shoulders pinch the tube at the neck of the bottle being filled and put this end into the next bottle and let the wine flow again.

As the level in the full jar falls, lower the tube into the wine. But be careful not to lower so far that the deposit begins to be sucked into the tubing. A good way of avoiding this is to ask a chemist to let you have fifteen inches of quarter-inch bore glass tubing and get him to bend the last inch of one end upwards. Then fit the straight end to the rubber tubing you have. At siphoning time, insert the glass tube to the bottom of the full jar of wine. The bend in the tube will rest on the bottom of the jar, but the opening of the end bent upwards will remain above the lees. Most friendly chemists will supply glass tubing at sixpence a foot and bend it for you free.

Now let me give the impatient wine-maker a warning. I know how nice it is to build up a stock and build it quickly, but don't be in such a hurry that you put wines away that are not yet perfectly clear. This results in disappointment upon opening if, as often happens, you decide to try a bottle of the oldest and the best you have for some special friend and find that you have stirred up a deposit and clouded what you imagined to be a perfectly clear wine. A reliable test to decide whether a wine is perfectly clear or not—and one I always carry out before bottling for storage purposes—is to hold a high-powered torch against the bottle.

If there is no suggestion of a beam passing through a haze, then the wine is as clear as you will get it; but if there is a slight beam of light, leave the wine to clear perfectly. You will soon get used to this little test and be saved from what might be a most embarrassing position.

Finally, when the clear wine has been bottled and the corks have been rammed home they should be sliced off level with the rim of the bottles. Sealing wax should then be run over the whole surface and the bottles stored on their sides.

Sealing and storing in this fashion is important because it allows for the wine to keep the cork moist and so prevent shrinkage. Shrinkage would cause cracking in the sealing wax with the result that tiny airholes would appear through which wild yeast and bacteria can attack the wine.

In the ordinary way a well-made wine—that is one made with good yeast and nutrient—is strong enough in alcohol to preserve itself. A goodly percentage of alcohol acts as its own preservative and that of the wine itself. But poorly made wines are low in alcohol and can be spoiled in the bottles if air reaches them. Our wine, made by the recipes and directions here, will contain enough alcohol to destroy any wild yeast or bacteria that might reach it owing to shrinkage of corks. Nevertheless, it is still important that air is not allowed to reach the wine, because if it did so for prolonged periods the quality would deteriorate, the flavour suffer and much of the bouquet be lost.

Experienced wine makers—myself included—use the new plastic seals which when fitted to a bottle of wine shrink tightly, effecting a perfect airtight seal. I expect you have come across these often enough on bottles of cordial. The T'Noirot extracts described in later chapters are fitted with these. When these capsules (as they are called) are used the bottles may be stored upright. Storing bottles horizontally often presents a problem for some people, but friends of mine with a small cupboard to spare have lined it with orange boxes. In each partition they have fitted soft-drinks cardboard crates so that each orange box holds twenty-four bottles on their sides. Having heard that wines must be stored at a temperature which should remain constant throughout the year, people are going to all sorts of trouble and thinking up all sorts of ingenious devices to achieve that end. Opinion is divided as to the ideal temperature in which to store wines—probably because wines, like human beings, prefer what suits them individually. The temperature suitable for one wine is not necessarily best for another.

Rapid changes of temperature are certainly best avoided, so if you can store your wines on a stone floor or in a cupboard which has a stone floor, so much the better. If you cannot do this, store your wines where you can and don't worry.

Maturing

I am afraid I always have to suppress a grin when people ask me how long a wine needs to mature because I know that all they really want to know is how soon they can drink it. It is surprising the number of people who simply will not believe that wines improve with age. They set about making wines possessed of an urgency which should not exist and an impatience that is hard to believe. They really believe that wine can be made, matured and drunk in six or seven weeks. With luck, you might get fermentation over and done with and your wines clear and bottled in that time, and truly they are drinkable even so young, but—and it is an enormous 'but'—wine tasted at that tender age cannot be compared with the same wine tasted a year later. It is impossible to describe the changes that take place, but take place they do. Chemical changes are taking place constantly, so that one batch of wine does not taste the same when sampled at intervals of six weeks.

I know full well that you will be itching to get your teeth into these wines and I cannot blame you for that—I'm the same myself, always anxious to sample the latest batch to be bottled off. And it is a waste of time for me to tell you to keep it at least a year before drinking because I know you'll never manage it; especially after you had a taste of it when siphoning it into bottles.

But please do this for your own sake. At bottling time, put, say, two bottles in the attic or some place where they cannot be reached easily—send them to me if you like. Seriously, those two bottles of each lot made will soon mount up to a nice little stock. The remaining four bottles from each gallon may be used as required.

The whole secret of building up a stock is to make several lots at the same time and when a jar is emptied at bottling time, start again with another lot. In this way you will always have a few gallons fermenting, several dozen bottles for use as required and a dozen or so slowly growing into a nice reserve. Then, when the first two bottles put away are a year or two old you may sample them. These will have become such magnificent wines in that time that your lesson will have been well and truly learned and the vow taken that henceforth half of all that is bottled is going to the attic. I hope it does, and I hope even more that you will be able to keep some of it for five years at least. For at five years it is better than age four and at three years old it is better than age two. I have proved all this to myself and have a few bottles of wine that I made over fifteen years ago. Must see what they're like, soon.

IMPORTANT BRIEFS

Fermentation Locks

There is no good substitute for the fermentation lock (described on page 22) and the one illustrated on page 23, is the best to use.

Many people use a balloon stretched over the jar instead of a fermentation lock, and provided this is a tight fit, it will certainly protect the wine. But this cannot give any indication as to when fermentation has ceased. The balloon is fitted over the neck and, as gas escapes into it, slight inflation takes place and as pressure grows the gas forces out round the neck of the jar.

Another substitute for the lock is a three-inch piece of quarter-inch bore glass tubing stuffed with cotton wool and fitted in the same way as the lock. But, as with a balloon, this can give no indication as to when fermentation has ceased.

Yeast—and adding it

It will be seen in the recipes that I give 'yeast' without mentioning any kind. This is because some of you will be using bakers' yeast and others one of the many varieties of wine yeast. In the directions which accompany the recipe, the time to add the yeast is clearly stated. If bakers' yeast is used, use half an ounce and crumble this into the jar at the time advised. Experienced wine makers and those using wine yeasts for the first time will have their little nucleus ferments ready (as instructed on page 17 under 'Aids to Fermentation') and these will be added at the time advised in the directions given with each recipe.

Sugar-Water (Syrup)

In the recipes and directions it will be seen that the sugar and water are added to the mixtures as a syrup. Make sure the sugar has dissolved before the water comes to the boil. And so that mistakes do not occur, label the jar so that you know how much sugar has to be added at each stage. There is no need to be exact when adding 'one-third' or whatever the direction happens to be, but it is a good plan to have the total amount of sugar to be used at the outset put aside; in this way, when all has been added you will know there is no more to go in and you will not be left wondering if you have used as much as you should have done.

Gallon Jars

Someone is sure to ask before they begin: How can I get a gallon of water, the flavouring, and all that sugar into a one-gallon jar? The fact is that, in the way we shall be doing it, it is quite a simple matter. Gallon jars hold half a pint more than a gallon when full, and because we shall be adding the sugar in stages, most of each lot of sugar will be used up before the next is added. Before the last lot of sugar and water is added, the wine is transferred to another jar and the deposit thrown away. This will leave space for the last lot of syrup to be added. If, through some misfortune, this is not quite the case, put the little remaining syrup in a freshly sterilized screw-stoppered bottle and screw down tightly. This will keep it safe for the few days necessary for fermentation to reduce the liquor in the jar and so make room for that little drop of left-over.

If at the time called for in the recipes you do not have a second jar in which to put the fermenting wine (at the time given for disposing of the deposit) you may pour the wine into any suitable container, then throw away the deposit, clean out the jar, sterilize it and then return the wine to this.

Saucepans

If it happens that your saucepans are not quite large enough to hold the sugar and five pints of water that is to be boiled at the first stage of making the wine, boil the sugar in a quart of water and the remaining three pints of water in another saucepan then mix.

CHAPTER TWO

Fresh fruit wines

THERE is no need for me to mention the enormous popularity this branch of home wine-making enjoys, or that countless thousands of people all over the world embark with tremendous enthusiasm each summer upon turning wild fruits and surplus garden fruits into wines fit to grace the tables of a banqueting hall. Just let me say that, no matter how advanced methods become and how easily obtainable special ingredients for wine making are, there will always be in the hearts of everyone a place for the true country wines, for they have that indefinable 'something' which sets them apart from all others, a uniqueness that cannot be found in any other wine either commercial or home produced.

The methods I use myself are described here, and although they are the simplest and the surest ever evolved, it is necessary to point out the complications that arise if these methods are *not* used.

Years ago—and, I am very sorry to say, even today—many thousands of unfortunate home wine makers are following methods which advocate: 'crush the fruits, add the water and leave to ferment'. Other methods advise boiling the fruits. In both cases disappointment is almost a certainty, and the reason for this is easy enough to understand.

The grey-white bloom that forms on grapes and other fruits is yeast put there by nature and it may be said that the first wine known to early man was the result of this yeast fermenting fruits crushed for a purpose other than wine-making. In the ordinary way, this yeast might well make good wine if allowed to ferment alone. Unfortunately, with this yeast comes what we term 'undesirable' yeast (wild yeast), and several kinds of bacteria—each of which can ruin our wines. They bring about what we call 'undesirable' ferments that usually take place at the same time as the ferment we *want* to take place so that instead of a wine of quality the resnlt is one tasting of flat beer or cloudy evil-smelling liquid fit only for disposal. Another bacterium, known as the vinegar bacterium, will turn wines into vinegar.

Since there is nothing we can do when any of these calamities has occurred, they must be prevented from happening.

Clearly, we must destroy all these enemies before beginning. The simplest method is of course—at first thought, anyway—is to boil the fruits. But here arises another problem. All fruits contain pectin, a glutinous substance which causes jams to 'set'. Boiling fruit releases pectin. This pectin holds itself and minute solids in suspension, giving the wine a cloudiness that is impossible to clarify or even filter out. We may put the crushed fruit through a jelly-bag to remove every particle of pectin-bearing fruit and then boil the juice only, but this is a messy, tedious job that takes hours and eliminates all the pleasure from wine-making.

Obviously, what we need is a method which will destroy the wild yeast and bacteria on the fruits (as boiling does) without actually boiling, and, indeed, without heating our fruits at all because it needs very little heat to bring out the pectin.

Our method, known as the 'sulphiting' method, does just this and produces full-bodied, crystal-clear wines easily and quickly without fuss or bother. All that is necessary to achieve this are tablets costing a ha'penny each. Campden fruit-preserving tablets are available at most chemists in bottles of twenty costing tenpence. In the ordinary way—

and provided the fruit is not too heavily affected with wild yeast and bacteria—one tablet will destroy the undesirable element contained in one gallon of crushed fruit pulp, but we cannot be sure of this. Now, two tablets will surely do this, but being a comparatively heavy dose this might also destroy the yeast we shall be adding so that the ferment we desire does not take place. My method takes care of both these risks, not only destroying the wild yeast and bacteria on the fruits, but also allowing the yeast we add to ferment alone and unhindered to produce wines of clarity and quality the like of which cannot be produced by any other method. By adding one Campden tablet to a good deal less than one gallon of fruit pulp ('must') this will represent a rough equivalent to two tablets per gallon. But before we add our yeasts we shall have increased the amount of liquid or pulp to nearly twice the amount, consequently reducing the amount of sterilizing solution to half or the equivalent of one Campden tablet per gallon. In this way we achieve our overall aim.

Each Campden fruit-preserving tablet contains four grains of sodium metabisulphite; therefore, any readers finding Campden tablets in short supply may ask their chemist for four grains of sodium metabisulphite (or potassium metabisulphite—there being two forms), and use this. But because a chemist would find a single order for four grains rather trivial, it would be best to ask for say, six or ten packets each containing four grains. If you are making two-gallon lots of wine the amount to use would be eight grains. Do not be tempted to buy by the ounce and measure out a grain as this is impossible unless you have the appropriate scales.

Just in case you happen to be one of those people who, even in these enlightened days, abhors the use of chemicals, let me assure you that sulphur dioxide (the solution which results when Campden tablets are dissolved) is quite harmless to humans when used in the proportions recommended. Indeed, as many as eight tablets (thirty-two grains) may be used with safety, but such heavy dosing would prevent a 'must' fermenting.

The sulphiting method is used by the trade, so we shall be following a method well tired and proved.

Heaven knows how many hundreds of gallons of wines I have made by this method and all with the same unfailing success.

Method 1 makes wines of the heavier type; their flavours are more pronounced and their colour more full than those produced by method 2. Those wishing for lighter wines more suitable for serving with meals should use method 2. The main difference in the two methods is that we ferment the fruit pulp itself in method 1, and the juice only in method 2. It will be appreciated that when fermenting the pulp we must as a matter of course get far more from our fruits. But we do not want too much in a light wine otherwise the subtle difference between a heavier wine and the popular lighter wines is lost.

The short pulp ferment of method 1 ensures that we get all the flavour and desirable chemical matter from our fruits in the right proportion.

The best method to use for each type of fruit is given with each recipe. It should be taken into account that varied amounts of fruit and sugar with the use of the proper method produce distinctly different types of wine.

Method 1

Crush the fruit by hand in a polythene pail and pour on one quart of boiled water that has cooled. Mix well. Crush one Campden tablet and dissolve the powder in about half an eggcupful of warm water and mix this with the fruit pulp. Leave the mixture for one or two hours. A little bleaching will take place but this is nothing to worry about.

After this, take one-third of the sugar to be used (or approximately one-third) and boil this for one minute in three pints of water. Allow this syrup to cool and then stir into the pulp. Then add the yeast (or nucleus) and ferment for seven days.

After seven days, strain the pulp through fine muslin or other similar material and wring out as dry as you can. Put the strained wine into a gallon jar and throw the pulp away. Then boil another one-third of the sugar in one pint of water for one minute and when this has cooled add it to the rest.

Plug the neck of the jar with cotton wool or fit a fermentation lock and continue to ferment in a warm place for a further ten days.

At this stage, if you have not a spare jar, pour the wine into the polythene pail leaving as much of the deposit in the jar as you can. Clean out the jar, sterilize it and return the wine to this.

The remaining one-third of the sugar may now be boiled for one minute in the remaining pint of water. When this has cooled, add it to the rest. Refit the lock or plug the neck of the jar with fresh cotton wool. After this, the wine should be left in a warm place until all fermentation has ceased.

Note. If there is not quite enough space for all of this last lot of syrup, put the remainder in a sterilized screw-top bottle and store for a few days in a cool place. This may be added when fermentation has reduced the level of the liquid in the jar. If you have to do this, don't forget to refit the lock.

Method 2

Crush the fruit in a polythene pail and add one quart of boiled water that has cooled. Mix well.

Crush one Campden tablet and dissolve the powder in about half an eggcupful of warm water and mix this with the fruit pulp. Leave the mixture in a cool place for twenty-four hours, stirring twice during that time. Strain through fine muslin or other similar material and squeeze gently but not too hard. Discard the fruit pulp.

Then boil one-third of the sugar in half a gallon of water for one minute and allow to cool. Mix this with the juice and return the lot to the polythene pail. Then add the yeast (or nucleus), and ferment for ten days.

After this, pour the top wine into a gallon jar leaving as much of the deposit behind as you can. Boil another one-third of the sugar in half a pint of water for one minute and when this is cool add it to the rest. Plug the neck of the jar with cotton wool or fit a fermentation lock and ferment in a warm place for fourteen days.

After this, boil the remaining sugar in the remaining half-pint of water for one minute and when this is cool add it to the rest. Refit the lock or plug the neck of the jar with fresh cotton wool and leave in a warm place until all fermentation has ceased.

The recipes are designed to make one gallon of wine, if two gallons are being made at once twice the amount of each ingredient must be used (including Campden tablets) and the sugar and water added in double quantities. This principle applies where three or four gallons are being made and it is easy enough to work out. Just to be sure that mistakes do not occur when adding the syrup—sugar and water—stick a label on the jar and note on this the amounts added.

Readers will be quick to appreciate that certain fruits are more suitable than others for making certain types of wine. Clearly, it would be as hopeless to try to make port from rhubarb as it would be to try to grow potatoes on a pear tree, and I think it is in this respect that many people go astray; they make wines from the cheapest and most readily available fruits (naturally enough) but they do not give the slightest thought to what the result will be or whether they will like it or not. Before you begin decide on the type of wine you are most likely to prefer and then use the fruit and the method which will make this type of wine.

Elderberries make an excellent port-style wine and many variations, each with the basic port style underlying them, so that from this lowly wild fruit we may obtain not only a full-bodied port-style wine, but also a Burgundy style, a claret and others according to the whim of the operator. Blackberries make similar wines, as do certain varieties of plums, damsons and blackcurrants. The juice from lighter-coloured fruit such as raspberries, loganberries, red and white currants and others make excellent table wines. But there is no need to cover this aspect fully here because every recipe is preceded by the name of the type or style of wine that can be expected from each recipe. I say 'expected', because to guarantee that the wine will be identical to the one expected would be unwise, but only because the amounts of sugar and acid present in the fruits vary from season to season—indeed, they vary with the type of tree, soil, situation and with the sort of summer we have had while the fruits have been growing. A hot dry summer produces fruits containing more sugar and less acid than a wet sunless summer, when the effect is the reverse.

In each recipe appears the name of the best yeast to use and this is best added as a nucleus as already described. If you must use bakers' yeast or a dried yeast, merely sprinkle it over the surface of the 'must' at the time given in the method you are using.

A final word. Make sure all fruits are ripe. This is far more important than most people imagine. Half-ripe fruits or those with green patches on them should be discarded as it needs only one or two of these in enough for a gallon of wine to give an acid bite to that wine. Fully ripe fruit is essential if we hope to make the best wine.

When you have decided that your garden fruits are ripe enough or those you have your eye on in the hedgerows, leave them for another three or four days before gathering.

BLACKBERRY WINE
Port Style

4 *lb. blackberries, 4 lb. sugar (or 5 lb. invert), 7 pts water, port yeast, nutrient.*

Use method 1. Ferment the pulp.

BLACKBERRY AND ELDERBERRY WINE
Port Style

2½ *lb. elderberries, 2½ lb. blackberries, 7 pts water, 3½ lb. sugar (or 4 lb. invert), port yeast, nutrient.*

Use method 1. Ferment the pulp after crushing and mixing together.

BLACKBERRY WINE
Burgundy Style

4–5 *lb. blackberries, 3¾ lb. sugar (or 4 lb. invert), burgundy yeast, nutrient, 7 pts water.*

Use method 1. Ferment the pulp.

BLACKBERRY WINE
Beaujolais Style

Wine made from this recipe won for me 1st prize among 600 entries on the occasion of the 2nd National Conference and Show of Amateur Wine-Makers at Bournemouth last year.

4½ *lb. blackberries*, 2½ *lb. sugar* (*or* 3 *lb.* 2 *oz. invert*), *burgundy yeast, nutrient,* 7 *pts water.*

Method 1 was used. The wine was, of course, dry.

BLACKBERRY WINE
Light Table Wine

3 *lb. blackberries*, 3 *lb. sugar* (3¾ *lb. invert*), 7 *pts water, burgundy yeast, nutrient.*

Use method 2. Ferment the diluted juice.

BLACKCURRANT WINE
Port Style

4 *lb. blackcurrants*, 1 *lb. raisins*, 3 *lb. sugar* (*or* 3¾ *lb. invert*), *port yeast, nutrient.*

Use method 1. Ferment the pulp with the raisins.

BLACKCURRANT WINE
Port Style

4 *lb. blackcurrants*, 7 *pts water*, 3½ *lb. sugar* (*or* 4 *lb. invert*), *port yeast, nutrient.*

Use method 1. Ferment the pulp.

BLACKCURRANT CLARET

3 *lb. blackcurrants, 2½ lb. sugar (or 3 lb. invert), 7 pts water, all-purpose wine yeast, nutrient.*

Use method 2. Ferment the diluted juice.

BLACKCURRANT WINE
A Light, Sweet Wine

3¾ *lb. blackcurrants, 3½ lb. sugar (or 4 lb. invert), 7 pts water, all-purpose wine yeast, nutrient.*

Use method 2. Ferment the diluted juice.

CHERRY WINE
A Delightful Sweet Wine

8 *lb. black cherries, 7 pts water, 3½ lb. sugar (or 4 lb. invert), all-purpose wine yeast or Bordeaux yeast, nutrient.*

Use method 1. Weigh with the stones and ferment the pulp.

CHERRY WINE
A Light Dry Wine

8 *lb. black cherries, 7 pts water, 2½ lb. sugar (or 3¼ lb. invert), sherry yeast is best, otherwise all-purpose wine yeast, nutrient.*

Use method 2. Ferment the strained diluted juice.

REDCURRANT WINE
Light Table Wine

3 *lb. redcurrants 7 pts water, 3 lb. sugar (or 3¾ lb. invert), all-purpose wine yeast, nutrient.*

Use method 2. Ferment the strained diluted juice.

REDCURRANT WINE
A Light Medium-Sweet Wine

4 *lb. redcurrants*, 7 *pts water*, 3½ *lb. sugar* (*or* 4 *lb. invert*), *all-purpose wine yeast*, *nutrient*.

Use method 2. Ferment the strained diluted juice.

DAMSON WINE
Port Style

8 *lb. damsons*, 7 *pts water*, 4 *lb. sugar* (*or* 5 *lb. invert*), *port yeast*, *nutrient*.

Use method 1. Weigh with the stones and ferment the pulp.

DAMSON WINE

Suitable for making into Damson Gin—see 'Recent Experiments', page 85.

5 *lb. damsons*, 7 *pts water*, 3 *lb. sugar* (*or* 3¾ *lb. invert*), *all-purpose wine yeast*, *nutrient*.

Use method 1. Weigh with the stones. Ferment the pulp.

DAMSON AND ELDERBERRY WINE
Port Style

3 *lb. damsons*, 1½ *lb. elderberries*, 3½ *lb. sugar* (*or* 4 *lb. invert*), *port yeast*, *nutrient*, 7 *pts water*.

Use method 1. Ferment the pulp.

DAMSON AND DRIED PRUNE WINE
Burgundy Style

Prunes should be soaked overnight, the water discarded and the prunes added in the crushed state to the crushed damson.

4 *lb. damsons, 2 lb. dried prunes, 7 pts water, 3 lb. sugar (or 3¾ lb. invert), burgundy yeast, nutrient.*

Use method 1. Ferment the crushed pulp.

RASPBERRY WINE
Light, Dry

4 *lb. raspberries, 2½ lb. sugar (or 3 lb. 2 oz. invert), 7 pts water, sherry yeast or all-purpose wine yeast, nutrient.*

Use method 2. Ferment the strained diluted juice.

RASPBERRY WINE
Sweet Dessert

4 *lb. raspberries, 1 lb. raisins, 7 pts water, 3½ lb. sugar (or 4 lb. invert), all-purpose wine yeast and nutrient.*

Use method 2. Ferment the strained diluted juice but with the chopped raisins for the first seven days.

ELDERBERRY WINE
Port Style

4 *lb. elderberries, 7 pts water, 4 lb. sugar (or 5 lb. invert) port yeast, nutrient.*

Use method 1. Ferment the crushed pulp.

ELDERBERRY WINE
Medium Dry

3½ *lb. elderberries, 3 lb. sugar (or 3¾ lb. invert), 7 pts water, sherry yeast or all-purpose wine yeast, nutrient.*

Use method 2. Ferment the strained diluted juice.

ELDERBERRY CLARET
Dry, of course

3 *lb. elderberries, 2½ lb. sugar (or 3 lb. invert), 7 pts water, sherry yeast or all-purpose wine yeast, nutrient.*

Use method 2. Ferment the strained diluted juice.

PLUM WINE
Burgundy Style

8 *lb. plums, any fully ripe red variety is suitable, 7 pts water* 3 *lb. sugar (or 3¾ lb. invert), burgundy yeast, nutrient.*

Use method 1. Weigh with the stones and ferment the crushed pulp.

PLUM WINE
Port Style

Dark red, fully ripe fruits must be used. 10 *lb. plums, 7 pts water, 3½ lb. sugar (or 4 lb. invert), port yeast, nutrient.*

Weigh with the stones.
Use method 1. Ferment the crushed pulp.

RHUBARB WINE

This wine is best made on the dry side and used as an appetizer. If you try to make it sweet, it would have to be rather too sweet. Four pounds of sugar will make it a medium sweet wine, but even this will not reduce the acidity which gives this wine its character and which, unfortunately, is causing it to lose its popularity. It is possible to remove the acid by using precipitated chalk, but this is hardly for beginners and a practice which, in any case, alters the whole flavour of the resulting wine.

5 lb. rhubarb, 3 lb. sugar (or 3¾ lb. invert), 7 pts water, sherry yeast or all-purpose wine yeast, nutrient.

Crush the rhubarb with a rolling pin, starting in the middle of each stick. Soak for five days in three pints of water (boiled), and in which one Campden tablet has been dissolved.

Then strain, wring out dry and warm just enough to dissolve half the sugar.

Having done this, ferment for ten days and then proceed as you would with any other recipe here, adding the rest of the sugar and water in stages.

LOGANBERRY WINE

3 to 4 lb. loganberries, 3 lb. sugar (or 3¾ lb. invert), burgundy yeast, nutrient, 7 pts water.

Use method 1. Ferment the crushed pulp.

Gooseberry Wine
Table Wine

6 *lb. gooseberries*, $3\frac{1}{2}$ *lb. sugar (or* $4\frac{1}{4}$ *lb. invert)*, 7 *pts water, tokay yeast or all-purpose wine yeast, nutrient.*

Use method 1. *But* ferment pulp for three days.

Gooseberry Wine
Sherry Style

The best gooseberries for this wine are those that have been left on the bushes to turn red or yellow, according to variety. They should be firm but soft and at the same time not damaged. Any damaged ones and any with a suggestion of mould or mildew on them must be discarded.

For a dry sherry style use $2\frac{1}{2}$ lb. sugar, for a medium dry use 3 lb., and for a medium sweet use $3\frac{1}{2}$ lb., or the corresponding amounts of invert sugar.

5 *lb. gooseberries*, 7 *pts water, sugar (as above), sherry yeast or all-purpose wine yeast, nutrient.*

Use method 1. But ferment the pulp for five days only.

Whortleberry Wine
Burgundy Style

Whortleberries are a small wild fruit which many people come to the country to pick; they make excellent jams and jellies—and very good wines, otherwise known as 'herts'.

6 *pts whortleberries*, 7 *pts water*, 3 *lb. sugar (or* $3\frac{3}{4}$ *lb. invert)*, *burgundy yeast, nutrient.*

Use method 1. Ferment the pulp.

WHORTLEBERRY WINE
Port Style

8 *pts whortleberries*, 7 *pts water*, 4 *lb. sugar (or 5 lb. invert)*, *port yeast*, *nutrient*.

Use method 1. Ferment the pulp.

WHORTLEBERRY WINE
Table Wine

5 *pts whortleberries*, 7 *pts water*, 2½ *lb. sugar (or 3 lb. 2 oz. invert)*, *all-purpose wine yeast*, *nutrient*.

Use method 2. Ferment the strained diluted juice.

SLOE WINE

Sloes make a delightful wine which is very popular with those living in the country, and is particularly suitable for turning into sloe gin. Not more than 4 lb. should be used owing to their astringency.

4 *lb. sloes*, 3 *lb. sugar (or 3¾ lb. invert)*, 7 *pts water*, *all-purpose wine yeast*, *nutrient*.

Use method 1. *But* ferment pulp for three days only.

CHAPTER THREE

Root wines

THE fame of these wines will never die. This is under-
standable when one considers that potatoes, parsnips and
carrots give you wines of superb character: wines that bear
striking resemblance to expensive spirits.

These wines are commonly known as 'carrot whisky' or
'potato Scotch' or whatever it is, and, make no mistake
about it, these wines do develop many of the characteristics
of whisky when kept a long time.

The first five recipes here make really good wines. Those
of you who want something quite exceptional and slightly
more expensive should use those recipes calling for the
addition of either wheat or raisins or both.

It will be seen that, in the recipes in this chapter, we add
oranges or lemons or both. The reason for this is that,
unlike fruit, roots contain no acid. Acid is essential to a
satisfactory ferment and for the purpose of improving the
flavour of the finished wines. But do not imagine that this
small amount of acid will make for an acid wine or that it
will be enough to give the wines the flavour of the oranges
or lemons—we shall not be using sufficient for that.

The ability to adjust the acid content of these wines so
easily—merely by adding the juice of an extra lemon or
orange—accounts to a large extent for their popularity. We
can make these wines with the absolute certainty that there
will not be the slightest astringency in them as sometimes
occurs in fruit wine made following a miserable summer or
when unripe fruits have been used. It is possible to test and
adjust the acid content of fruit mixtures, but this involves

the use of costly laboratory equipment and some experience in laboratory technique if it is to be accurate. By sticking to the recipe, you are assured that the varying acid contents of fruit have been allowed for and that the wines will not be over acid except under the most abnormal circumstances. The necessary acid is given to the root wines by the lemons and oranges. Two lemons contain the equivalent of a quarter-ounce of citric acid. Therefore, if it is more convenient to use this by all means do so, and add this at the time you would add the juice of the lemons. You should, however, use the oranges as well where called for as their flavour is required, whereas only the acid of the lemons is necessary.

For trouble-free root wine-making it is best to use old roots, that is, main crop that have been stored. These contain less starch than the fresher roots. Starch boiled into the liquid at the start will remain in the finished wine if we are not careful. There is no easy means of removing starch cloud from wines, filtering will not shift it. A starch-destroying enzyme may be used, but this is not for the beginner; the best plan therefore is to avoid the presence of too much starch. The reason for this is that if the yeast has too much sugar and starch to cope with it will not handle either properly. But by adding the sugar in stages, the yeast will not be overworked and will convert the starch to sugar and then to alcohol. But if there is too much starch and too much sugar the result will be a pea-soup-like wine.

When making wines from potatoes it is best to wait until May or early June when the last of the previous year's main crop is nearly exhausted and if these have long sprouts on them it will not matter provided the sprouts are rubbed off before the potatoes are used. Do not use any roots with damp patches on them. Parsnips that have had a couple of October frosts make good wines and if they have had these frosts while lying on the soil, so much the better.

Small shrivelled carrots which have lost their hardness make the best carrot whisky while the last of the stored beetroot makes the best beetroot wines. Another factor to consider when using old roots is that we do not get what is often termed an 'earthy' flavour into the wines. Fresh mangolds may be used. These are a winter food for cattle and are available from farms from October onwards. Two shillings worth of mangolds (mangel-wurzels) will make about five gallons of one of the nicest of pale-gold wines. Turnips and swedes—well, I am sorry, I have heard of people who have made something with these roots, but I must confess that friends and I who have carried out trials with them have been forced to conclude that while they *might* make good wines, we have not had much success with them, and we have decided that with so many other kinds of material available it is hardly worth while wasting time trying to evolve a reliable recipe for each of these roots.

Note

The sulphiting process advised for making fruit wines is not suitable for making root wines. Nor is any method that does not call for actually boiling the roots. Wines made from roots that are not boiled almost always have an unpleasant after-taste or 'tang' and often give rise to stomach upsets.

When using recipes calling for wheat and raisins, it must be borne in mind that these must be sterilized before being added to the 'must'. See note and method of sterilizing under the heading 'Grain Wines and Wines from Dried Fruit', page 104. Also explained under this heading is the reason for adding tea when making wines with the recipes in this chapter, tea being added to most of the recipes which do not include raisins. When straining hot liquids or solids, as we shall be, it is a good plan to tie one cloth on to the fermenting vessel (polythene pail), allowing sufficient sag, and then to put another piece over this. This will enable you to lift off the top cloth containing the solids without having to go to the bother of trying to untie the string while at the same time trying to prevent the weight of the solids dragging them into the strained liquor.

Clearing root wines. In the ordinary way root wines, like all wines, begin to clear as soon as fermentation loses its vigour, but, of course, no wine can become perfectly clear in the sense that it is perfectly clear for bottling until all fermentation has ceased. This is because the agitation of fermentation is certain to keep minute solids in suspension if only to give a slight haze. As I have already mentioned earlier, even a clear wine has some deposit to throw.

When fermentation has ceased, root wine usually becomes clear in stages. The top inch becomes clear in a matter of days, and then within a few days of fermentation having ceased the top half of the wine is usually brilliantly clear and later on you will be able to observe that what appears as a flat-topped fog bank is slowly settling to the bottom, leaving brilliant wine above·it. The fog bank I have described may be of three or four densities, the bottom being heavy deposit, those layers above being lighter so that the top one is but a fine mist.

As with other wines, it is best to let these have their own way and clear of their own accord, which they will do in time —usually within a week or two even if you happen to encounter a slow clearing.

However, if you are in a hurry or if that cloud seems slower than usual in settling, you can help it by using isinglass.

One ounce of isinglass from a chemist will cost about one and sixpence. Take a little of the wine and crumble about one-eighth of an ounce for each gallon of wine to be treated over the surface of this and warm it gently in an enamel saucepan, stirring until the isinglass is dissolved. Then pour this milk into the bulk. This should clear the wine very quickly, but it might still take several days.

Bakers' yeast and household sugar are used in these recipes, and you will find the results far above your expectations.

The reason for using five quarts of water in these recipes is that we are using enough ingredients for a gallon of wine, and because we shall finish up with one gallon. If we used only one gallon of water we would end up with about three quarts of wine because about a quart will be lost during boiling and other operations.

Be sure to remove any scum that rises while the roots are being boiled—this is most important.

EASY POTATO WINE

2 lb. potatoes, 1 lb. raisins, 4 oranges, 4 lb. sugar, 1 oz. yeast, nutrient, 5 qts water.

Scrub and grate the potatoes and put them in half a gallon of water. Bring slowly to boiling point and simmer for one minute, and then strain into the fermenting vessel. Add half the sugar at once and stir until all is dissolved. Then put in the cut-up raisins and cut-up oranges and peel. Allow to cool and then add the yeast. Cover as directed and ferment for ten days. Then strain, wring out dry.

Boil the rest of the water and sugar together for one minute and when cool add this to the rest. Then put into a gallon bottle and cover as directed again or fit fermentation lock and leave until all fermentation has ceased.

Wine made with the above recipe is especially suitable for turning into potato gin. See page 87.

EASY PARSNIP WINE

2 lb. parsnips, ½ lb. raisins, 2 oranges, 2 lemons, 4 lb. sugar, 5 qts water, 1 oz. yeast.

Scrub and grate the parsnips and simmer them gently for five minutes in three quarts water—taking off all scum that rises. Strain and add half the sugar at once and stir until all is dissolved. Then put in the cut-up raisins and cut-up oranges and lemons and their peel. Allow to cool and then add the yeast.

Cover as directed and ferment for ten days. Then strain and wring out as dry as you can. Boil the rest of the sugar and water together for one minute and when cool add this to the rest. Then put into a gallon bottle and cover as directed or fit fermentation lock and leave until all fermentation has ceased.

PARSNIP WINE

4 lb. parsnips, 4 oranges, 3½ lb. sugar, 5 qts water, 1 oz. yeast.

The above makes an excellent imitation of whisky, but to achieve this it must be kept for a long time.

The preparation of ingredients and directions for making this wine are identical with those for making easy parsnip wine (see above).

MANGOLD WINE

Known in country areas as mangel-wurzel wine, this is a true favourite. The mangolds may be obtained from farms from October until the end of April.

5 *lb. mangold (usually one medium-size root)*, 2 *lemons*, 2 *oranges*, 4 *lb. sugar*, 5 *qts water*, 1 *oz. yeast*.

Do not peel the mangold, scrub it thoroughly and cut it into thin slices or dice it, being careful not to lose any juice. Bring to the boil and simmer gently in half a gallon of water for fifteen minutes.

Then strain on to two pounds of sugar in the fermenting vessel, stirring until all the sugar is dissolved. Then add the cut-up oranges and their peel. Allow to cool and then add the yeast. Cover as directed and ferment for ten days.

Then strain out the oranges and squeeze dry. Boil the rest of the sugar and water together for two minutes and when cool add this to the rest. Put into a gallon jar and cover as directed or fit fermentation lock and leave until all fermentation has ceased.

Note

If there appears to be insufficient water while simmering use more but keep account of how much is used and reduce the amount to be added later on accordingly.

BEETROOT WINE

5 *lb. beetroot*, 2 *oranges*, 2 *lemons*, 4 *lb. sugar*, 5 *qts water*, 1 *oz. yeast*.

Peel the beetroots, slice them finely being careful not to lose any juice. Put them in three quarts water and bring to the boil, simmering gently for not more than ten minutes. Strain into the fermenting vessel and add half the sugar, stirring until all is dissolved. Then cut up and add the oranges and lemons and their peel. Allow to cool, then sprinkle the yeast on top. Cover as directed and ferment for ten days. Then strain out the oranges and lemons and wring out dry.

Boil the rest of the water and sugar together for two minutes and when cool add this to the rest. Put into a gallon jar. Then cover as directed or fit fermentation lock and leave until all fermentation has ceased.

MIXED-ROOT WINES

Mixtures of roots make excellent wines as those who have mixed odd drops of various wines will confirm. Indeed, it is mixing odd drops of wine that gives people ideas for recipes. They think that a certain mixture of potato and parsnip wine really is delightful, and so a new recipe is born. They decide to make the blend by using half of each of the ingredients used in each wine and make a good job of it.

The following mixtures have all been tried and proved reliable, and all may be worked to the directions given for making easy parsnip wine on page 56.

Recipe 1
2 lb. potatoes, 2½ lb. carrots, 2 oranges, 2 lemons, 3½ lb. sugar, 1 oz. yeast, 5 qts water.

Recipe 2
2 lb. potatoes, 2½ lb. parsnips, 2 oranges, 2 lemons, 4 lb. sugar, 1 oz. yeast, 5 qts water.

Recipe 3
2½ lb. carrots, 2½ lb. beetroots, 2 oranges, 2 lemons, 4 lb. sugar, 1 oz. yeast, 5 qts water.

Recipe 4
2½ lb. carrots, 2 lb. parsnips, 4 oranges, 2 lemons, 4 lb. sugar, 1 oz. yeast, 5 qts water.

Recipe 5
2 *lb. potatoes*, 2½ *lb. beetroots*, 2 *oranges*, 2 *lemons*, 4 *lb. sugar*, 1 *oz. yeast*, 5 *qts water*.

JUNGLE JUICE

The following recipe is an improved version of a recipe which is known in every corner of this country as 'Bravery's Extra Special Fine Old Jungle Juice'. That recipe, having been offered to readers of Noël Whitcomb's column of the *Daily Mirror*, brought no fewer than 30,000 requests. And today, five years later, it is acclaimed by individual correspondents and wine-making clubs everywhere. The Secretary of the Coventry Circle writes: 'Bravery's Jungle Juice is a well-famed liquor that has delighted many a member's throat and palate.'

3 *lb. old potatoes*, 6 *oranges*, 1 *lb. raisins*, 1 *lb. wheat*, 4 *lb. sugar* (*do not use invert*), 1 *oz. yeast*, 5 *qts water*.

Use very old potatoes. See note on ingredients at the beginning of this chapter.

Cut up the oranges and their peel and boil them gently for three minutes in three pints of water. Then stand this aside to cool. Do not peel the potatoes, but scrub them thoroughly. Then grate or slice them finely and bring them to the boil in six pints of water. Simmer gently for not more than ten minutes, taking off all scum that rises. If scum continues to rise at the end of ten minutes simmering, continue simmering until no more rises, taking off every bit of it.

Strain into a polythene pail and add half the sugar at once, stir until dissolved. Then add the wheat and cut-up raisins. Then add the oranges and the water in which they were boiled. While the liquid is still lukewarm, sprinkle the yeast on top and stir in.

Ferment for ten days.

After this, strain out the solids and return the liquor to the fermenting vessel.

Then boil the rest of the sugar in the remaining pint of water and when cool add this to the rest.

Continue to ferment in a warm place for a further ten days when it should be put into jars under fermentation locks or covered as directed and left in a warm place until all fermentation has ceased.

CARROT WHISKY

The valuable contribution of Noël Whitcomb, the famous columnist of the *Daily Mirror*.

6 *lb. carrots*, 1 *gal. water*, 1 *tablespoonful raisins*, 1 *!lb. wheat*, 1 *oz. yeast*, 2 *oranges*, 2 *lemons* 4 *lb. sugar*.

Scrub the carrots clean—don't peel them—and mash them. Put them in the water, bring to the boil and simmer gently until tender. Then strain off the liquid (you can use the carrots for food—most dogs love them). Into the fermenting vessel put the sugar and sliced lemons and oranges and pour the hot liquid over them. Stir until the sugar is dissolved and stand until lukewarm. Then add the chopped raisins and wheat and sprinkle the yeast on top. Leave to ferment for fifteen days, then skim, strain and bottle.

To get the fullest flavour, keep it for nearly a year—if you can.

CHAPTER FOUR

Ribena wine

BEFORE I explain how easy it is to make wine with Ribena let me point out that this famous syrup of excellent quality could well be added to fermenting 'musts' made up from other fruits to get special results. The rate to add it would be one to two bottles per gallon.

When making wines from dried fruits the addition of one or two bottles of Ribena per gallon would make a vast improvement to the flavour and quality of the wine. Similarly, when making wines from fresh fruits that give a red wine, one or two bottles of Ribena could well be added to make up for other fruits if they happen to be in short supply. If you use Ribena in this way, you may disregard the SO_2 preservative (more about this later) because the amount in the Ribena will not be enough to stop fermentation, but it would be best to add it at the vigorous fermentation stage—during the first ten days.

If you propose to use Ribena in this way, bear in mind that each bottle contains approximately eight ounces of sugar, so you should reduce accordingly the amount of sugar in whichever recipes you are using.

Undiluted Ribena is not readily fermentable, because it contains just over seven pounds of sugar per gallon and is preserved with 350 parts per million SO_2—either of which is capable of preventing fermentation.

Obviously, our aim when making wine with Ribena will be to reduce the amount of sugar to about three and a half pounds per gallon, by using half Ribena and half water. In doing this, we shall reduce the SO_2 preservative to around

175 parts per million. This amount is unlikely to prevent fermentation, though it could do so.

My trials with Ribena were carried out with the above points borne in mind and it will be seen that I began with a good deal less than equal parts of Ribena and water, gradually bringing them up to equal parts.

Because I did not want to overwork the yeast by giving it too much sugar to work on at the start, and because I wanted to reduce the SO_2 content to below 175 parts per million (without heating with the risk of spoiling the flavour of the syrup), I decided to work to the following method. This method, incidentally, met with the approval of V. L. S. Charley, B.SC., PH.D., technical director of the Royal Forest factory of the Beecham group and one-time director of the Long Ashton Research Station, Bristol.

All water used in the process was first boiled and allowed to cool naturally.

Stage 1

Two bottles of Ribena were diluted with twice the amount of water (four Ribena bottles full). Yeast in the form of a nucleus was added and the mixture allowed to ferment for ten days.

Stage 2

After ten days' fermentation, two bottles of Ribena and one Ribena bottle of water were added and the mixture allowed to ferment for a further ten days.

Stage 3

After a total of twenty days' fermentation, two bottles of Ribena and one more bottle of water were added. Fermentation was then allowed to carry on to completion, taking, in all, three months.

The result was a good, round wine flavoured delightfully but not too strongly of fresh blackcurrants.

At stage 3 it was borne in mind that, while most of the SO_2 would have been driven off during fermentation by adding those last two bottles, I was, in effect, bringing the total SO_2 content up to 175 parts per million. Fearing that the yeast might be just a little weakened at this stage I decided to drive off the SO_2 in the last two bottles by raising the temperature of them to $70°$ C. If you want to do this and have no suitable thermometer, stand the bottles in a saucepan of water and slowly raise the temperature until the Ribena in the bottles has increased in volume enough to reach the rims of the bottles. The temperature is high enough to drive off the SO_2 and the heat should be cut off at once. The caps of the bottles must be removed before heating. The whole of fermentation was carried out in narrow-necked bottles plugged with cotton wool, fermentation locks being fitted after ten days. Racking was not carried out until one month after the last addition. Monthly racking followed until fermentation ceased. Even at this early stage the wine was nice to drink, but it had improved vastly at the age of six months.

At first it might seem expensive to make wine with Ribena, but against the cost one should set the fact that no sugar need be added and that one has a top-quality product all ready for the job in hand. Apart from this, there is no expensive fruit to buy, no messy crushing—in fact nothing much to do at all. And, most important of all, Ribena has been treated with a pectin-destroying enzyme, which means that you could boil it if you wished without fear of pectin clouding the finished wines. Such boiling would, of course, drive off the SO_2 and give you a wine flavoured slightly of cooked blackcurrants.

For the benefit of experienced readers who use the hydro-meter, Ribena has a specific gravity of 1·283.

It will be seen that a sweeter wine may be made by using one bottle more of Ribena or one less of water, while a dry wine would result if less Ribena were used. A dry wine would lack the fuller flavour, but this would be offset to some extent by the dryness.

If eight bottles of Ribena are made into one gallon by adding water, that gallon will contain roughly four pounds of sugar and the equivalent of four pounds of blackcurrants. This amount of fruit is ample for a gallon of wine and, provided one likes a fairly sweet wine, this proportion of sugar to fruit is not too much. On the whole, I feel that seven bottles of Ribena would be the limit you could use to make a gallon of wine without it being too sweet.

It will be clear that my trials with Ribena, using six bottles to make just under one gallon of wine, have been most successful and I do urge readers to have a go.

A point to bear in mind is that a good light wine is often made with as little as two pounds of blackcurrants to the gallon, therefore, if you made four bottles of Ribena into a gallon of 'must', you would have used the equivalent of two pounds of blackcurrants and two pounds of sugar. This would give you a wine of about twelve per cent of alcohol by volume. Such a wine would be dry, but by adding half a pound of sugar during the process you would get a sweeter wine of one or two per cent more alcohol.

CHAPTER FIVE

Wines from prepared extracts

THIS chapter shows how easily wines the flavour of world-famous liqueurs and other commercial products may be made with the minimum of utensils and labour; indeed, this is probably, if not decidedly, the simplest, the least troublesome and the most rewarding of all adventures into wine-making.

In what are known as T'Noirot Extracts we have a readily prepared ingredient and, as will be seen in the recipes, no preparation is needed, the stuff is ready to use.

You might get a decent imported wine or British wine at seven and six a bottle, but you will never be able to buy wines with the flavour of these world-famous liqueurs at any price, and certainly not for three shillings a bottle—all they will cost you to make. Nor will you ever buy Vermouth at less than fifteen shillings a bottle; the Vermouth recipe alone, then, must be worth a fortune to anybody who likes Vermouth.

When making these wines do please use a good yeast and nutrient, for the results obtained in this way will surpass any you can hope to achieve by using bakers' yeast and no nutrient.

It will be seen in the recipes that I have included invert sugar because this give the best results here. Invert sugar contains a little acid and this is essential in wine-making as we have already seen. If you use household sugar, you will have to add the juice of one lemon or one-eighth ounce of citric acid to give just the tiny amount of acid required.

When adding the extract to the prepared syrup (sugar-water), make sure you get all of it out of the bottles.

When deciding which extract to use, you must first decide on which you are likely to prefer (unless you know in advance and from experience that you like Vermouth or Kirsch or cherry brandy) and then choose that one. In this way you will not make a wine that might disappoint you—after all, not all tastes are the same.

Important

The method we shall be using calls for adding these very highly concentrated flavourings to a very small amount of liquid to begin with. The flavour will be very, very strong, so do not sample it, and the odour given off might strike people as not quite pleasant. This is quite natural, so do not be put off using them because of this. And don't take a 'sniff' of the wine during the early stages, for the same reason.

T'Noirot Extracts—and what they are made of

The following list contains the names of most of the T'Noirot Extracts that we shall be using in this chapter and beside each appears details of their contents. The extracts are scientifically blended to give flavours identical to the world-famous liqueurs of the same names. Thus you are assured of the real thing and not a synthetic substitute.

These flavourings are highly concentrated and should not, therefore, be judged by their odour. Anyone smelling the raw undiluted material or sampling the wines made from the extracts is likely to imagine that something is not quite right. Do not pay any attention to the strength or pungency of the odour and do not sample any wines being made from the extract until fermentation has almost ceased. Even at this stage it is not wise to try to judge the wine. Wait, I implore you, until fermentation has ceased altogether and the wine has been clear for at least a month. As with all other wines, the flavour improves immensely with age. I am able to speak from first-hand experience because I have been making wines with these extracts, and I can assure you in absolute sincerity that each extract makes a wine identical in flavour to the world-famous commercial liqueur the name of which it carries.

And let me just add that the oil of juniper mentioned in other parts of this book is an extract of juniper berries—juniper being an ornamental shrub grown a good deal in this country.

Liqueur Green Convent	Both distilled from plants
Liqueur Yellow Convent	growing in the high mountain regions. These two established the now world-wide reputation of T'Noirot.
Curaçao, red	Two liqueurs of Dutch origin
Curaçao, white	distilled from small green oranges.
Cherry brandy	Made from unfermented cherries.
Danzig	A liqueur of German origin.
Kümmel	Of continental origin, extracted from caraway seeds. Wine made from this extract would act as a stimulant of the digestive organs.
Mirabelle	Distilled from the famous Lorraine plum.
Prunelle	Distilled from the wild plum.

Many of these extracts contain blends of bitter and aromatic plants—Vermouth being a good example of this. We are all well aware of the delicate flavours of the French and Italian Vermouths and will thus be enabled to appreciate the value of all the T'Noirot Extracts, for they bring us something quite unique when it comes to making wines from them.

These extracts were not intended for the purpose to which I put them. Making wines from them instead of fruit or other ingredients is my own idea entirely and I am proud to be the originator of both the idea and of the recipes herein. I am also proud to pass them on to my readers all over the world.

As will be seen in the recipes, I have advised carrying out the entire fermentation in the gallon jar, but if you would prefer to ferment for the first ten days in a polythene pail by all means do so, but make certain it is covered as directed earlier. If you do this, give the liquor a good stir before putting it into the jar otherwise some of the deposit and a lot of flavouring may be lost. Do not on any account divide the liquor, say, into two half-gallon lots because half-gallon jars happen to be available. Keep it as one until all fermentation has ceased. When this has happened the clearer wine may be siphoned off the deposit into another jar and put away to clear. When clear, it should be bottled.

CHERRY BRANDY WINE

6 bottles of cherry brandy extract, 3 lb. sugar (or 3¾ lb. invert), 1 gal. water, yeast and nutrient.

Boil one-third of the sugar in half a gallon of water for two minutes, allow to cool and pour into the gallon jar. Then add the extract, yeast and nutrient.

Cover as directed or fit fermentation lock and ferment in a warm place for ten days. Then boil another third of the sugar in a further quart of water for two minutes and when cool add this to the rest. Cover again as before or refit the lock and continue to ferment in a warm place for a further fourteen days.

After this, boil the rest of the sugar in the remaining quart of water as before and when cool add to the rest. Cover again or refit the lock and leave in a cool place until all fermentation has ceased.

VERMOUTH (ITALIAN)

6 *bottles of Italian Vermouth extract*, 3 *lb. sugar (or* 3¾ *lb. invert), yeast and nutrient.*

Boil one-third of the sugar in a half-gallon of water for two minutes. Allow to cool and pour into a gallon jar. Then add the extract, yeast and nutrient.

Cover as directed or fit fermentation lock and ferment in a warm place for ten days. Then boil another one-third of the sugar in a further quart of water and when this is cool add it to the rest. Cover again or refit the lock and continue to ferment in a warm place for a further fourteen days. After this, boil the remaining sugar in the remaining quart of water as before, when cool add to the rest. Cover again or refit the lock and leave in a warm place until all fermentation has ceased.

VERMOUTH (FRENCH)

6 *bottles of French Vermouth extract*, 3¼ *lb. sugar (or* 4 *lb. invert)*, 1 *gal. water, yeast and nutrient.*

Boil one-third of the sugar in half a gallon of water for two minutes and when cool pour into a gallon jar. Then add the extract, yeast and nutrient.

Cover as directed or fit fermentation lock and ferment in a warm place for ten days. Then boil another one-third of the sugar in a quart of water for two minutes and when cool add this to the rest. Allow to ferment in a warm place for a further fourteen days.

After this, boil the remaining water and sugar as before and when cool add to the rest.

Cover again or refit the lock and continue to ferment in a warm place until all fermentation has ceased.

CREAM OF APRICOT WINE

5 bottles of cream of apricot extract, 3 lb. sugar (or 3¾ lb. invert), 1 gal. water, yeast and nutrient.

Boil one-third of the sugar in half a gallon of water for two minutes, allow to cool and pour into a gallon jar. Then add the extract, yeast and nutrient.

Cover as directed or fit fermentation lock and ferment in a warm place for ten days. Then boil another third of the sugar in a quart of the water for two minutes and when this is cool add it to the rest. Cover again as directed or refit fermentation lock and continue to ferment in a warm place for a further fourteen days.

After this, boil the rest of the sugar in the remaining water as before and when cool add to the rest. Cover again or refit the lock and continue to ferment in a warm place until all fermentation has ceased.

CREAM OF PEACH WINE

6 bottles of extract of cream of peach, 3 lb. sugar (or 3¾ lb. invert), 1 gal. water, yeast and nutrient.

Boil one-third of the sugar in half a gallon of water for two minutes and when cool pour into a gallon-size glass jar. Then add the extract, yeast and nutrient.

Cover as directed or fit fermentation lock and ferment in a warm place for ten days.

Then boil another one-third of the sugar in a quart of water and when cool add this to the rest. Cover again as directed or refit the lock and continue to ferment in a warm place for a further fourteen days.

After this, boil the rest of the sugar in the remaining water as before and when cool add to the rest. Cover again as directed or refit the lock and continue to ferment in a warm place until all fermentation has ceased.

SLOE GIN WINE

6 bottles of sloe gin extract, 3 lb. sugar (or 3¾ lb. invert), 1 gal. water, yeast and nutrient.

Boil one-third of the sugar in half a gallon or water for two minutes and when cool pour into a gallon jar. Then add the extract, yeast and nutrient.

Cover as directed or fit fermentation lock and ferment in a warm place for ten days. Then boil another one-third of the sugar in a quart of water as before and when this is cool add it to the rest. Cover again or refit the lock and continue to ferment in a warm place for a further fourteen days.

Then boil the rest of the sugar in the remaining water as before and when cool add to the rest. Cover again or refit the lock and continue to ferment in a warm place until all fermentation has ceased.

RATAFIA WINE

6 *bottles of Ratafia extract*, 3 *lb. sugar (or* 3¾ *lb. invert*), 1 *gal. water, yeast and nutrient*.

Boil one-third of the sugar in half a gallon of water for two minutes and when cool pour into a gallon glass jar. Then add the extract, yeast and nutrient.

Cover as directed or fit fermentation lock and ferment in a warm place for ten days. Then boil another one-third of the sugar in a quart of water as before and when this is cool add it to the rest. Cover again or refit the lock and continue to ferment in a warm place for a further fourteen days.

After this, boil the rest of the sugar in the remaining water as before and when cool add to the rest.

Cover again as directed or fit fermentation lock and continue to ferment in a warm place until all fermentation has ceased.

KIRSCH WINE

6 *bottles of Kirsch extract*, 3 *lb. sugar (or* 3¾ *lb. invert*), 1 *gal. water, yeast and nutrient*.

Boil one-third of the sugar in half a gallon of water for two minutes and when cool pour into a gallon glass jar. Then add the extract, yeast and nutrient.

Cover as directed or fit fermentation lock and ferment in a warm place for ten days.

Then boil another one-third of the sugar in a quart of

water as before and when this is cool add it to the rest. Cover as directed or refit the lock and continue to ferment in a warm place for a further fourteen days.

After this, boil the remaining sugar in the rest of the water as before and when cool add to the rest. Cover again as directed or refit the lock and continue to ferment in a warm place until all fermentation has ceased.

MIRABELLE WINE

6 bottles of Mirabelle extract, 3 lb. sugar (or 3¾ lb. invert), 1 gal. water, yeast and nutrient.

Boil one-third of the sugar in half a gallon of water for two minutes and when cool pour into a gallon glass jar. Then add the extract, yeast and nutrient.

Cover as directed or fit fermentation lock and ferment in a warm place for ten days. Then boil another one-third of the sugar in a quart of water as before and when this is cool add to the rest. Cover again or refit the lock and ferment in a warm place for a further fourteen days.

After this, boil the remaining sugar in the rest of the water as before and when cool add to the rest.

Cover again as directed or refit the lock and continue to ferment in a warm place until all fermentation has ceased.

PRUNELLE WINE

6 bottles of Prunelle extract, 3 lb. sugar (or 3¾ lb. invert), 1 gal. water, yeast and nutrient.

Boil one-third of the sugar in half a gallon of water for two minutes and when cool pour into a gallon glass jar. Then add the extract, yeast and nutrient.

Cover as directed or fit fermentation lock and ferment in a warm place for ten days. Then boil another one-third of the sugar in a quart of water as before and when this is cool add it to the rest. Cover again or refit the lock and continue to ferment in a warm place for a further fourteen days.

After this, boil the remaining sugar in the rest of the water as before and when cool add to the rest.

Cover again or refit the lock and continue to ferment in a warm place until all fermentation has ceased.

MARASQUIN WINE

6 *bottles of Marasquin extract, 3 lb. sugar (or 3¾ lb. invert), 1 gal. water, yeast and nutrient.*

Boil one-third of the sugar in half a gallon of water for two minutes and when cool pour into a gallon glass jar. Then pour in the extract, yeast and nutrient.

Cover as directed or fit fermentation lock and ferment in a warm place for ten days. Then boil another one-third of the sugar in a quart of water for two minutes and when cool add this to the rest. Cover again or refit the lock and continue fermenting in a warm place for a further fourteen days.

After this, boil the remaining sugar in the rest of the water as before and when cool add to the rest. Cover again or refit the lock and continue to ferment in a warm place until all fermentation has ceased.

MANDARINE WINE

6 *bottles of Mandarine extract, 3 lb. sugar (or 3¾ lb. invert) 1 gal. water, yeast and nutrient.*

Boil one-third of the sugar in half a gallon of water for two minutes and when cool pour into a gallon glass jar. Then add the extract, yeast and nutrient.

Cover as directed or fit fermentation lock and ferment in a warm place for ten days. Then boil another one-third of the sugar in a quart of water as before and when cool add this to the rest. Cover again or refit the lock and continue to ferment in a warm place for a further fourteen days.

After this, boil the remaining sugar in the rest of the water as before and when cool add to the rest.

Cover again or refit the lock and continue to ferment in a warm place until all fermentation has ceased.

GREEN CONVENT WINE

5 *bottles of Green Convent extract, 3 lb. sugar (or 3¾ lb. invert), 1 gal. water, yeast and nutrient.*

Boil one-third of the sugar in half a gallon of water for two minutes and when cool pour into a gallon glass jar Then add the extract, yeast and nutrient.

Cover as directed or fit fermentation lock and ferment in a warm place for ten days. Then boil another one-third of the sugar in a quart of water as before and when cool add this to the rest. Cover again or refit the lock and continue to ferment in a warm place for a further fourteen days.

After this, boil the remaining sugar in the rest of the water as before and when cool add to the rest. Cover again or refit the lock and continue to ferment in a warm place until all fermentation has ceased.

YELLOW CONVENT WINE

5 *bottles of Yellow Convent extract, 3 lb. sugar (or 3¾ lb. invert), 1 gal. water, yeast and nutrient.*

Boil one-third of the sugar in half a gallon of water for two minutes and when cool pour into a gallon glass bottle. Then pour in the extract, yeast and nutrient.

Cover as directed or fit fermentation lock and ferment in a warm place for ten days. Then boil another one-third of the sugar in a further quart of water and when this is cool add it to the rest. Cover again as before or refit fermentation lock and continue to ferment in a warm place for a further fourteen days.

Then boil the remaining sugar in the rest of the water as before and when cool add to the rest.

Cover again as directed or refit fermentation lock and continue to ferment in a warm place until all fermentation has ceased.

Reverendine Wine

6 bottles of Reverendine extract, 3 lb. sugar (or 3¾ lb. invert), 1 gal. water, yeast and nutrient.

Boil one-third of the sugar in half a gallon of water for two minutes and when cool pour into a gallon glass jar. Then add the extract, yeast and nutrient.

Cover as directed or fit fermentation lock and ferment in a warm place for ten days. Then boil another one-third of the sugar in a quart of water as before and when this is cool add it to the rest.

Cover again as before or refit fermentation lock and continue to ferment in a warm place for a further fourteen days.

After this, boil the remaining sugar in the rest of the water as before and when cool add to the rest. Cover as directed or refit the lock and continue to ferment in a warm place until all fermentation has ceased.

Red Curaçao Wine

6 *bottles of Red Curaçao extract, 3 lb. sugar (or 3¾ lb. invert), 1 gal. water, yeast and nutrient.*

Boil one-third of the sugar in half a gallon of water for two minutes and when cool pour into a gallon glass jar. then add the extract, yeast and nutrient.

Cover as directed or fit fermentation lock and ferment in a warm place for ten days. Then boil another one-third of the sugar in a quart of water as before and when cool add this to the rest. Cover again as directed or refit fermentation lock and continue to ferment in a warm place for a further fourteen days.

After this, boil the remaining sugar in the rest of the water as before and when cool add to the rest. Cover again or refit the lock and continue fermenting in a warm place until all fermentation has ceased.

White Curaçao Wine

6 *bottles of White Curaçao extract, 3 lb. sugar (or 3¾ lb. invert), 1 gal. water, yeast and nutrient.*

Boil one-third of the sugar in half a gallon of water for two minutes and when this is cool pour into a gallon glass jar. Then pour in the extract, and add the yeast and nutrient.

Cover as directed or fit fermentation lock and ferment in a warm place for ten days. Then boil another one-third of the sugar in a quart of water as before and when cool add this to the rest. Cover again or refit the lock and continue to ferment in a warm place for a further fourteen days.

Then boil the remaining sugar in the rest of the water as before and when cool add to the rest. Cover again as before or refit fermentation lock and leave in a warm place until all fermentation has ceased.

Kümmel Wine

6 *bottles of Kümmel extract*, 3 *lb. sugar (or* 3¾ *lb. invert)*, 1 *gal. water, yeast and nutrient.*

Boil one-third of the sugar in half a gallon of water for two minutes and when cool pour into a gallon glass bottle. Then add the extract, yeast and nutrient.

Cover as directed or fit fermentation lock and ferment in a warm place for ten days. Then boil another one-third of the sugar in a quart of water as before and when this is cool add to the rest.

Cover again or refit fermentation lock and continue to ferment in a warm place for a further fourteen days.

After this, boil the rest of the sugar in the remaining water as before and when cool add to the rest. Cover again or refit the lock and put in a warm place until all fermentation has ceased.

Danzig Wine

6 *bottles of Danzig extract*, 3 *lb. sugar (or* 3¾ *lb. invert)*, 1 *gal. water, yeast and nutrient.*

Boil one-third of the sugar in half a gallon of water for two minutes and when cool pour into a gallon glass bottle. Then pour in the extract and add the yeast and nutrient.

Cover as directed or fit fermentation lock and ferment in a warm place for ten days. Then boil another one-third of the sugar in a quart of water as before and when this is cool add it to the rest. Cover again as before or refit fermentation lock and continue to ferment in a warm place for a further fourteen days.

After this, boil the remaining sugar in the rest of the water as before and when cool add to the rest.

Cover again as directed or refit the lock and continue to ferment in a warm place until all fermentation has ceased.

EAU-DE-VIE WINE

5 bottles of extract of Eau-de-Vie, 3 lb. sugar (or 3¾ lb. invert), 1 gal. water, yeast and nutrient.

Boil one-third of the sugar in half a gallon of water for two minutes and when cool pour into a gallon glass bottle. Then add the extract, yeast and nutrient.

Cover as directed or fit fermentation lock and ferment in a warm place for ten days. Then boil another one-third of the sugar in a quart of water as before and when cool add this to the rest. Cover again as before and continue to ferment in a warm place for a further fourteen days. After this, boil the remaining sugar in the rest of the water as before and when cool add to the rest.

Cover again as directed or re-fit fermentation lock and continue to ferment in a warm place until all fermentation has ceased.

CHAPTER SIX

Wines for the ladies

Preserved, Sweet or Dry Wines of Low Alcohol Content

IT is mostly men who want their wines to be knock-out
drops and usually they take care to get them as strong as
possible. But a high percentage of alcohol is not everything.
Many—indeed, I would say most—continental wines are
in the region of eight to eleven per cent of alcohol. Ours,
made with the recipes in this book, will be a good deal
stronger than this as has already been explained. It is the
ladies who like the milder-flavoured, low-alcohol, dry to
medium-dry or medium-dry to sweet wines, so let me explain how any recipe here may be quite easily turned into
a 'wine for the ladies'.

Mentioned in earlier chapters is the fact that a good percentage of alcohol ensures that wines keep well, and that
the lower-alcohol wines—those under twelve per cent—
might begin fermenting again at any time. This is because a
stray yeast spore, either left in the wine or one reaching it
at some later stage, will begin to reproduce and live on any
sugar present. Only the very driest of low-alcohol wines will
keep and these must be so dry that no unfermented sugar
remains at all.

However, not everybody likes bone-dry wines; most
people prefer them medium dry to medium sweet or even
sweet.

The wines made with the recipes in this book will keep
well provided the maximum alcohol has been reached, and
if all directions have been followed this will have been
achieved. They will keep because they contain enough

alcohol to destroy any yeast or bacteria that may reach them.

Our aim when making low-alcohol wines is to add just enough sugar to make the amount of alcohol required and to allow the wine to ferment right out, and this it will do of its own accord. The wine will be dry if less than two and a quarter pounds of sugar are used for one gallon.

Now take a look at the short table on page 83. This shows the amount of sugar needed to produce the amount of alcohol required in one gallon of wine; if two gallons are being made the amount of sugar required would have to be doubled.

Let us suppose we have decided on making a wine of ten per cent of alcohol: the amount of sugar to add is approximately one pound fourteen ounces per gallon.

Very well then, take any recipe in this book (but not those containing dried fruit as these contain quite a lot of sugar) and instead of using the amount of sugar given in that recipe, use one pound and fourteen ounces instead.

As already mentioned, the resulting wine will be bone dry—too dry even for those fond of the drier wines. To reduce this dryness we may sweeten to taste either by adding dissolved invert sugar (which dissolves quite readily) or by dissolving household sugar in some of the wine in the following manner. Care must be taken here to ensure that the wine does not come into contact with metals. One pint of wine from one gallon will do. Put this into a china jug or similar vessel and stand this in a saucepan of water. Add, say, one teaspoonful of sugar for each bottle (one gallon, six bottles) and warm the water until the sugar in the wine is dissolved. Mix this with the bulk and sample. If this is not quite sweet enough, you will know that the process may be repeated. If you are using invert sugar, the sugar itself may be dissolved in an enamel saucepan and the resulting syrup stirred into the wine.

Very well, we now have a low-alcohol wine with sugar in it. To prevent it fermenting at some later date we may preserve it without harming it in any way.

Here again, Campden tablets play their part, but if the wine is crystal clear, Campden tablets might cloud it slightly. This should settle out, but it would mean that re-bottling might be necessary when this had happened. It is better therefore to use four grains of potassium metabisulphite in place of one Campden tablet. This should be enough to preserve one gallon of wine.

Crush the bisulphite crystals, and dissolve them in a little warmed wine and stir this into the bulk immediately after sweetening. Make sure the crystals are quite dissolved. I have written that one Campden tablet (or four grains of bisulphite crystals) *should* preserve a gallon of wine—and so it should, but under exceptional circumstances it might not. One more tablet (or four more grains of bisulphite crystals) may be added without harmful effects, except that it might give just a hint of flavour to the most delicately flavoured wines—though it will not affect those with a good all-round flavour. Fortunately, there is a simple test that we may carry out to decide whether a second tablet is needed or not.

First, pour a little of the treated wine into a wine-glass and bung down the remainder. Cover the glass with a small piece of cloth and leave in a warm room (not a hot place), overnight or for eight to twelve hours. Note carefully the colour when setting it out and again the following morning (or compare this sample with a sample freshly drawn from the bulk). If darkening of the sample left overnight has occurred, then an extra tablet is needed. If darkening has not occurred, one tablet (four grains metabisulphite) has done the job, and you have a low-alcohol wine of required dryness or sweetness that will keep well.

Up to 450 parts SO_2 are allowed by law in 1,000,000 parts wine, and this is represented by approximately eight Campden tablets (or thirty-two grains potassium metabisulphite). Two tablets (eight grains) represent just over one hundred parts per million; so it will be seen that we are not, after all, using very much.

Dry wines finish fermenting sooner than wines of a higher alcoholic content because there is less sugar to be fermented out.

This preserving of wines may be carried out with all wines if you wish, whether they be high-alcohol wines or not.

Sugar		Potential alcohol
lb.	oz.	per cent
1	4	7·6
1	8	9·2
1	14	10·8
2	0	12·3

The above figures refer to the use of household sugar.

If invert sugar is being used, it must be borne in mind that this contains some moisture, so that for every pound of household sugar one must use one and a quarter pounds of invert sugar. So that mistakes do not occur, I have included the amounts of each sugar to use so that you may choose for yourself which to use and know how much of either—*not* both.

Invert sugar is usually supplied in tins containing seven pounds or in blocks by whatever weight is ordered. If weighing this proves awkward, dissolve it and measure it by the pint, bearing in mind that one pint represents two pounds of sugar.

CHAPTER SEVEN

Recent experiments

GIN WINES

I AM especially glad to be able to pass on the results of my most recent experiments. The gin recipes here were evolved from a single idea. I wanted to make a wine as near as possible in taste to commercial gin, and because gin has no colour worth mentioning my first thoughts were to ferment sugar and water and flavour the resulting 'wine'. But I was aware that yeast produces more alcohol when the fermenting liquor contains the essentials of yeast reproduction—that is, in addition to sugar and nutrient, it needs also a vegetable matter such as fruit pulp. But all fruits and most vegetables give colour to wine and my aim was to produce a strong wine with little or no colour at all. Potato wine always turns out a good strong wine and since this has no colour I decided to carry out trials with potatoes, and made my first potato-gin wine.

During these experiments I evolved complete recipe ; however, there is no need to put them here because replicas of them appear in other parts of this book. All you need to know is how to get the gin flavour in the various wines to which this addition is specially suitable.

In case you feel like experimenting on your own here, I had better mention that it is useless to add the oil of juniper to a fermenting 'must' because it will separate from the rest and be lost during one of the various operations. Even when this is added to the finished wines it will separate because there is not enough alcohol to keep it in solution. But this does not matter all that much because we are still able to get the fragrant gin flavour we are after.

Mind you, we shall not be able to make wines *identical* to gin because gin is a spirit and we cannot produce that amount of alcohol. The only way we could do this would be to add gin to these special wines and since I am concerned in giving you wines costing only a few shillings a gallon, I would prefer that you forget the idea of adding gin unless you really do feel it worth while. Some of you will, of course, and if you do it should be added to the clear finished wines. The amount you add will depend only on the depth of your pocket.

The orange and lemon gin wines here will be stronger than the popular gin and orange served over the bar. This is because a single gin is usually diluted with twice its amount of orange or lemon cordial. Therefore, the 70° proof of the gin is diluted to about 23° proof. Ours will be a bit stronger than this; about 30° proof provided we use a good yeast and nutrient and get the maximum alcohol. But whereas the orange or lemon gin served over the bar is clouded by the cordial ours will be clear wine.

Now, the whole point is this: we add the oil of juniper to get the flavour of gin in a finished wine and, because it separates to form a fine film on the surface, the bottle must be shaken a little before the wine is served. Therefore, the oil of juniper must not be added until the wine is perfectly clear and when there is no suggestion of a deposit in the bottles—which, of course, would be disturbed by the shaking.

Finally, don't add oil of juniper for the sake of novelty to any wine; make sure first that you will like the result.

As much or as little of the oil may be added according to taste, and it is better to experiment with one bottle of the

chosen wine rather than the gallon; in this way only one
bottle is involved if you decide after all that one particular
type of gin wine is not to your liking.

Sufficient oil of juniper to flavour several gallons of wine
may be had from any chemist for about two shillings. Use
an eye-drop dispenser, adding the oil drop by drop,
sampling after each addition until you get the strength of
flavour you like. I find five drops to the gallon about right,
or one to the bottle, but your preference may be very
different from mine.

Suitable recipes to be made into gin wines are: the
potato wine recipe on page 55; the orange wine recipe on
page 88; the lemon wine recipe on page 89; the damson
wine recipe on page 45; the sloe wine recipe on page 50.

Gin and Peppermint Wine

This makes a very good imitation of the popular 'gin
and pep'.

Make the potato wine on page 55. When it is finally a
clear, finished wine, flavour with peppermint essence and
oil of juniper. Do this carefully otherwise the effect will be
ruined.

CHAPTER EIGHT

Wines from citrus fruits

Make these wines with bakers' yeast—fresh.

ORANGE WINE

This is a delightful wine that develops a flavour that can readily be likened to an orange-flavoured whisky.

12 *large oranges, or their equivalent,* 4 *lb. sugar,* ½ *oz. yeast,* 1 *gal. water, nutrient.*

Drop the whole oranges into boiling water, and push each one under the surface. Then take them out and throw the water away.

Cut the oranges into small pieces and pour over them half a gallon of boiled water that has cooled. Cover well, and leave to soak for forty-eight hours, crushing and pressing the peel between the fingers to extract the oil which gives a very special flavour. Then boil half the sugar in a quart of water for two minutes and when cooled add this to the orange pulp. Then add the yeast and nutrient. Ferment this in a warm place for five days. Then crush, strain through fine muslin or other suitable material and wring out dry. Discard the pulp and return the fermenting liquor to the fermenting vessel, and allow to ferment for a further ten days. Carefully pour off into a gallon jar, leaving as much of the deposit behind as you can.

Then boil the rest of the water and sugar together and when cool add to the rest. Then fit fermentation lock or cover

as directed and continue to ferment in a warm place until
all fermentation has ceased.

LEMON WINE

This wine is not ordinarily made to drink as a wine. It is
often made by experienced wine makers for blending with
dried fruit wines which sometimes fall short of acid require-
ment. But more often it is made as a novelty. It is particularly suitable for making into lemon gin wine.

Use the above directions for making orange wine—using
eight lemons instead of using oranges.

GRAPEFRUIT WINE

This is another acid wine, but many people like it, especially where a pound of raisins or dates are fermented with the
grapefruits.

Use eight large grapefruits following the orange wine
recipe above. If you wish to add a pound of raisins or
dates do so as soon as you have cut up the grapefruits and
ferment them with the rest for the first few days—until
straining time.

Note

If raisins or dates are used, use half a pound less of
sugar, because dried fruits contain approximately fifty per
cent sugar.

TANGERINE WINE

This makes a really delightful wine and as many tangerines
may be used as suits you—but do not use less than fifteen
or more than thirty.

Dates or raisins may be used with this as well as in the

grapefruit recipe and the notes about this should be followed if you want to add them. However, I feel that you would find the raw fruits more to your liking.

Follow the directions for orange wine on page 88 when making tangerine wine.

CHAPTER NINE

Flower wines and miscellaneous recipes

LET me begin this chapter by assuring you that one of the loveliest wines I have ever tasted was made with gorse flowers by a member of the Bournemouth Wine-Makers' Circle. This I sampled while lecturing at the Town Hall there on the occasion of the Amateur Wine-Makers' Second Annual Conference and Show.

Flower wines, cannot, of course, be likened to any other homemade wine—or commercial wine—because their flavours are unique; they can only be described as delicately aromatic, their bouquet cannot be found in any other wine.

Their popularity is lessened only by the labour of collecting the flowers; but by choosing a spot where they abound, enough for a gallon or two may be gathered in an hour.

Care is needed if we are to get the best from our ingredients. When gathering the flowers it is best to use a basket of ample size because crushing will damage the flowers and we shall not get such a delightful wine.

All flowers should be gathered on a dry day but not necessarily on a sunny one; though it *must* be sunny when collecting dandelions otherwise they are either closed or half-closed and difficult to find. In their closed state they teem with insects which would get into the wine and spoil it. Dandelions close when gathered but this does not matter. In fact it is a great help because we should use only the petals of dandelions, and when they are closed the petals may be pulled out all together merely by holding the head of the flower and pulling on the petals grouped together.

Although only petals should be used many people make quite a good dandelion wine by using the whole heads, but I use petals only.

To achieve the best result a wine yeast should be used and this may be an all-purpose wine yeast. Invert sugar should not be used in these recipes because it is inclined to slightly alter the aroma of the flower and change the delicate colour of the wines made from recipes in this chapter.

Bakers' yeast is included in the recipe together with household sugar; those preferring to use a wine yeast 'started' as directed may, of course, do so.

GORSE WINE

5 pts gorse flowers, 3 lb. sugar, 1 gal. water, 1 oz. yeast. Five pints is the minimum amount of gorse flowers to use, you may use more if you wish—up to one gallon if you can get them Other ingredients would remain the same.

Put the flowers in the fermenting vessel and pour on half a gallon of boiling water. Cover and leave to soak for three days, stirring each day and covering again at once.

Boil half the sugar in a quart of water for two minutes and when this is cool add to the flower mixture. Then add the yeast and ferment for three days.

Strain out the flowers and continue to ferment the liquor in the fermenting vessel for a further seven days.

Then pour into a gallon jar, leaving as much of the deposit behind as you can. Boil the rest of the sugar in the remaining water for two minutes and when cool add to the rest.

Cover as directed or fit fermentation lock and continue to ferment until all fermentation has ceased.

Note

Many people prefer this when the juice of one lemon is added at the same time as the yeast.

CLOVER WINE
(Use only Mauve Clover)

3 qts clover heads, 2 lemons, 3 lb. sugar, 1 gal. water, 1 oz. yeast.

Pull off the petals by gathering them between the fingers whilst holding the base of the flower head. Put the petals in the fermenting vessel and pour on half a gallon of boiling water. Leave well covered for twelve hours.

Boil half the sugar in a quart of water for two minutes and when cool add this to the rest. Then add the yeast and ferment the mixture for seven days.

Strain out the flowers, but do not squeeze too hard, and put the liquor into a gallon jar. Then boil the rest of the sugar in the remaining water and when cool add this to the rest. Cover as directed or fit fermentation lock and leave until all fermentation has ceased.

DANDELION WINE

1 gal. flower heads without the tiniest piece of stalk, 3 lb. sugar, 1 oz. yeast, 1 gal. water, 2 lemons.

Remove petals as directed for clover wine. Put the petals in the fermenting vessel and pour on three quarts of water—boiling and leave to soak for seven days, well covered.

Stir daily, and cover again at once. Strain and wring out fairly tightly and return the liquor to the fermenting vessel. Boil half the sugar in a pint of water and when cool add to the liquor, then add the yeast and the juice of two lemons.

Cover as directed and ferment for seven days. Then pour carefully into a gallon jar, leaving as much deposit behind as you can. After this, boil the rest of the sugar in the remaining pint of water and when cool add to the rest. Cover as directed or fit fermentation lock and leave until all fermentation has ceased.

COLTSFOOT WINE

1 gal. coltsfoot flowers, 3 lb. sugar, 1 gal. water, 1 oz. yeast.

Pull the petals off in the same way as for dandelions.

The method for making this wine is identical to the recipe for making dandelion wine on page 93.

HAWTHORN BLOSSOM WINE

2 qts of the flowers, 3½ lb. sugar, 1 oz. yeast and 1 gal. water.

Gathered when the flowers are about to drop they may be shaken off into the fermenting vessel.

The method for making this wine is identical to the recipe for making dandelion wine on page 93.

ELDER FLOWER WINE

1 gal. flower, 1 gal. water, 3½ lb. sugar, 1 oz. yeast, 2 lemons.

Boil half the sugar in half a gallon of water and while boiling pour over the flowers in the fermenting vessel. Add the juice of the lemons and when the mixture is cool add the yeast. Cover as directed and ferment for seven days.

Strain out the flowers and wring out well, but not too dry. Put the strained liquor in a gallon jar.

Boil the rest of the sugar and water for two minutes and when cool add to the rest. Cover as directed or fit fermentation lock and leave until all fermentation has ceased.

Another very good elder flower wine may be made in exactly the same way as the above using only five pints of the flowers with three pounds of sugar, two lemons, 1 oz. yeast and one gallon water.

ROSE PETAL WINE

One of the most delightful of all flower wines. The petals of roses of various colours may be used in one lot of wine, but if you have enough of, say, both red and yellow for a separate lot of each, do keep them separate.

3 qts rose petals (*strongly scented if possible*), 1 gal. water, 3 lb. sugar, 1 oz. yeast, 2 lemons.

Pour half a gallon of boiling water over the petals in the fermenting vessel, cover well and leave for forty-eight hours, stirring often.

Boil half the sugar in a quart of water for two minutes and when this is cool add to the petal mixture and ferment for three days.

Strain and wring out well, and return the liquor to the fermenting vessel and let it ferment for a further ten days.

Pour the liquor into a gallon jar, leaving as much of the deposit behind as you can. Then boil the rest of the sugar and water as before and when cool add to the rest together with the juice of the lemons. Cover again as directed or fit fermentation lock and leave until all fermentation has ceased.

TEA WINE

Many wine-makers save left-overs from the teapot until they have enough to make a gallon of wine, but I find that the flavour of the wine is somewhat impaired when this is done. Better to make a gallon of weak tea and to start straight off. Don't be tempted to make strong tea for this purpose otherwise you will have too much tannin in the wine.

8 teaspoonfuls of tea, 1 gal. water, 1 lb. raisins, juice of 2 lemons, 3 lb. sugar, 1 oz. yeast.

Make tea in the ordinary way using eight teaspoonfuls and a quart of water. Let it stand undisturbed for ten minutes, and then strain into the fermenting vessel.

Boil half the sugar in half a gallon of water for two minutes and when cool add this to the tea. Then add the raisins and finely sliced lemons and their juice. Add the yeast and ferment for ten days, stirring daily. Strain into a gallon jar. Then boil the rest of the sugar in the remainder of the water for two minutes and when cool add this to the rest. Cover as directed or fit fermentation lock and leave to ferment in a warm place until all fermentation has ceased.

IMITATION TIA MARIA

I am not fond of this myself, but I know of a good many people who are and who make this wine quite regularly.

The best plan is to make either easy potato wine or easy parsnip wine as on pages 55–6, and when this has ceased fermenting flavour it with freshly made coffee or one of the proprietary brands of essence. But do this very carefully as it is easy to overdo it, thus spoiling the flavour.

ROSE HIP WINE

One of the finest of all home-made wines; its flavour is unique and it has body and bouquet that take a lot of matching. Rose hips abound in early autumn and it matters not whether they are gathered from your own rose trees or from the hedgerows. They should not be used until they have taken on their winter coat of red or orange according to the type.

4 *lb. rose hips*, 3 *lb. sugar*, 1 *gal. water*, 1 *oz. yeast*.

Wash the hips well in half a gallon of water in which one Campden tablet has been dissolved. Crush the hips with a mallet or chop them. Put them in the fermenting vessel and pour on half a gallon of boiling water. Boil half the sugar in a quart of water for two minutes and when cooled a little add to the rest. Add the yeast and ferment the pulp for seven days.

Then strain out the solids and put the strained liquor into a gallon jar. Boil the rest of the sugar in the remaining water for two minutes and allow to cool well before adding to the rest. Cover as directed or fit fermentation lock and leave to ferment in a warm place until all fermentation has ceased.

CHAPTER TEN

Wines from dried herbs

IN case the advantages of making wines from dried herbs do not immediately become evident, let me explain that the town and city dweller (and countryman, too, for that matter) may make all the old favourite wines of Granny's day for next to nothing. Practically no work is involved because, unlike fresh fruits which have to be gathered and roots that have to be scrubbed, grated and boiled, suitable packets of herbs are available ready for use. In any case, many town and city dwellers might well know of the old country wines and wish that they could make them—indeed, they may well have lived in the country and tasted the wines made from the fresh herbs; dandelion, sage, coltsfoot, mint, balm, yarrow and countless others.

People living in large towns like Coventry and Birmingham have written to me asking about this field of wine-making, for they recall their early days when 'Mum' used to make what they now describe as 'really wonderful wines from leaves she used to collect from the fields all round where we used to live'.

Dried herbs normally cost less than two shillings per packet and such a packet is usually more than enough for a gallon of wine. The actual amount of the dried article may be varied according to personal tastes, but usually two ounces is enough for one gallon, and this amount rarely costs more than eighteen pence. I have found that the packets of herbs supplied by Heath and Heather Ltd., of St. Albans, Hertfordshire (branches in many towns), are usually suitable for one gallon of wine—though the amount in each packet varies slightly with the variety of herb.

Those who know their herbs well enough to gather them fresh from the garden or field or hedgerow may do so, of course, but it must be borne in mind that one needs at least one pound of the fresh plant to get the equivalent of two ounces of the dried. It is most important one should be expert at identification because many health-giving herbs bear a striking resemblance to others which have proved themselves to be deadly poisonous. By buying ready packeted herbs such risks are done away with, and Heath and Heather Ltd. will send to anyone free on application their book of herbs.

In some of the recipes which follow the addition of raisins or wheat, or both, is recommended, and while I would stress that their use is quite optional, I do strongly advise readers to use them where they are specified unless they know in advance that they prefer wines made without them. The use of raisins or wheat, or both, adds body and bouquet where these properties may be lacking. As you will have guessed, the herb gives only flavour—apart from its known medicinal properties—and some aroma, but does not give the same amount of bouquet as a fully flavoured fruit; wheat and raisins help in this respect. As with root wines, the addition of acid is necessary and this may be added as citric acid at the rate of a quarter-ounce per gallon or as the juice or two large lemons—whichever suits you best.

A nutrient is also necessary for the same reasons as have already been described early in this book.

The amounts of sugar in the recipes are those generally used, but readers now know that they make their herb wines dry merely by reducing the amount of sugar according to their wishes.

It should be borne in mind that while we use a gallon of water, and while the sugar occupies space at the rate of a quart to every four pounds, we shall arrive back at the gallon of wine aimed at because there will be some loss during boiling, loss of most of the sugar which will be fermented out and some small wastage when transferring to other bottles. A little less sugar is used in these recipes as compared with fresh fruit wines; this is because there is no acidity or astringency to balance, as is often the case where fruit wines are made.

The amounts of herbs given in the recipes are the amounts usually used and I advise readers to use them to begin with. Later, say when fermentation has nearly ceased, they may sample for strength of flavour; if they feel they would like it stronger, a little more of the herb may be added, but this should not be necessary.

On the other hand, if the flavour happens to be a little too strong a pint or two of boiled and cooled water may be added to dilute the strength of flavour. This will increase the overall amount of wine so that the amount of sugar added will not be enough for the increased amount. Therefore, when boiling the additional water, boil with it three to four ounces of sugar to each pint and then add this syrup slowly, taking samples until the strength of flavour is right. The recipes in this chapter have been given me by friends. The trials I have carried out with them have proved most satisfactory and I know readers will be pleased with the results. As will be seen, most recipes call for two ounces of the herb, but it will be found that the one-and-sixpenny packets of dried herbs from Heath and Heather will suffice in all but exceptional cases, where, for example, a very strong flavour is required. Where kola nuts are used, a tenpenny packet is enough.

All dried herbs may be obtained from most chemists, but sometimes their stock is likely to be a little old. Heath and Heather deal in this field to such a large extent that their herbs can be relied upon to give the best results. Alternatively get them from a reliable herbalist if you have one in your locality.

The following method is suitable for all recipes in this chapter.

Lemons and oranges should be peeled, the fruit broken up and added and the peel discarded.

Method

Put all the ingredients (except sugar and yeast) in a polythene pail and pour on half a gallon of *boiling* water. Leave for two to three hours covered as directed. Then boil half the sugar in a quart of water for two minutes and add this to the rest while still boiling. Mix well, and when cool enough add the yeast and nutrient. Cover again and ferment in a pail in a warm place for ten days, stirring daily and covering again at once.

After ten days, strain out the solids and wring out as dry as you can, and put the strained liquor into a gallon glass bottle. Boil the other half of the sugar in the remaining quart of water for two minutes and when cool add this to the rest. Cover as directed or fit fermentation lock and continue to ferment in a warm place until all fermentation has ceased.

BALM WINE

2 oz. dried balm leaves, 2 lemons, 3 lb. sugar, 1 gal. water, yeast and nutrient.

PARSLEY WINE

2 oz. dried parsley, 1 oz. dried mint (or ½ oz. fresh mint), ½ oz. dried sage (red), 1 gal. water, 2 oranges, 2 lemons, 3 lb. sugar (or 3¾ lb. invert), yeast and nutrient.

BROOM WINE

2 oz. dried broom flowers, 2 lemons, 1 lb. raisins, 2½ lb. sugar (or 3¼ lb. invert), yeast and nutrient.

DAMIKOLA WINE

2 oz. dried damiana leaves, 1 oz. kola nuts, ½ oz. dried red sage, 1 lb. raisins, 3 lb. sugar (or 3¾ lb. invert), 2 lemons, 1 gal. water, yeast and nutrient.

SAGE WINE

3 oz. dried sage, 1 lb. raisins, 1 oz. dried mint, 1 lb. wheat, 2 lemons, 2½ lb. sugar (or 3¼ lb. invert), yeast and nutrient.

YARROW WINE

2 to 3 oz. of dried yarrow flowers, 2 lemons, 2 oranges, 3 lb. sugar (or 3¾ lb. invert), 1 gal. water, yeast and nutrient.

CLARY WINE

3 to 4 oz. clary flowers, 1 lb. raisins, 2 lemons, 3 lb. sugar (or 3¾ lb. invert), 1 gal. water, yeast and nutrient.

BURNET WINE

3 oz. burnet herb, 1 lb. raisins, 1 lb. wheat, 2 oranges, 2 lemons, 3 lb. sugar (or 3¾ lb. invert), 1 gal. water, yeast and nutrient.

I do strongly advise you to experiment with half-gallon lots of these wines and to add tiny amounts of aniseed or liquorice as fermentation nears completion. If you do this with varying amounts of herbs you must not let the total weight of the herbs exceed four ounces to the gallon of wine being made. I realize, of course, that a beginner cannot have any definite plan for blending because he will not be familiar with the flavours given to the wines by the various herbs. If you accidentally spoil the flavour of a wine by trying to improve it, you may dilute with sugar-water, and while fermentation is still going on, add other herbs to get the flavour you are aiming at. If you happen to find that the flavour is not quite strong enough you may suspend a bag of herbs in the fermenting 'must' until you get the strength of flavour you want. And this may be tested at few-day intervals by tasting.

No matter how many years you may have been making wines and no matter how many different varieties you have made, it will be clear from the number of recipes in this book that there are plenty you have not tried your hand at. However, do not be tempted to make thirty or forty different varieties on a grand scale. Make, say, half a dozen bulk lots with recipes and fruit you are familiar with, and experiment with half-gallon lots. In this way you will always have a nice stock and if any particular experiment goes wrong or perhaps does not turn out quite as hoped, little will be lost.

CHAPTER ELEVEN

Wines from dried fruits and grain

THE making of wines from grain and dried fruits is a boon to the townsman who finds these ingredients easily obtainable and they make good wines. Mixtures of dried fruit and grains make for strong, fully flavoured, but not too fully flavoured wines which, when not made too sweet, are often likened to whiskies and brandies. They need time to mature to reach their best—two years is not too long, though at one year old they are very excellent wines. As with root wines the addition of some acid is necessary here (see 'Root Wines', chapter three), and this is put into the 'must' in the form of oranges and lemons.

Most dried fruit is heavily sulphited to prevent fermentation, and most wheat or other grain has been in contact with all sorts of dirt, dust and bacteria. Therefore they must be well cleansed before use. Break up the raisins and drop them into boiling water. As soon as the water boils again cut off the heat, strain the raisins and throw the water away. The raisins are then ready for use. Do the same with the wheat or other grain, but use a separate saucepan; they are then ready for use.

Tannin

Most recipes for fruit wines allow for tannin in the fruits to be given into the 'must'. This tannin forms an important part of the flavour of the wine—though few people realize it. But they soon know when there is too much because the wine takes on the flavour or 'tang' of strong, unsweetened tea. The little tannin given to fruit wines is usually just the right amount.

In the ordinary way there is no tannin present in dried fruit wines. Therefore it is as well to add one tablespoonful of freshly made tea—not too strong—to make good this deficiency. Special grape tannin is available, but tea is a cheap and handy source of which we might as well make use.

The addition of tea is included in the recipes.

CANADIAN WHISKY

2 lb. wheat, 2 lb. raisins, 1 lemon, 4 oranges, 3 lb. sugar, 1 oz. yeast, 5 qts water, 1 tablespoonful of freshly made tea.

Boil half the water with half the sugar for one minute and then pour on the wheat and raisins. Put the lot into the fermenting vessel and squeeze in the juice of the lemon. Cut up the oranges and their peel and put these with the rest. Work the orange peel between the fingers to press out the oil—much flavour is obtained from this.

When cool add the yeast and ferment for ten days. Then strain out the solids and wring out as dry as you can and put the strained liquor into a gallon jar with a tablespoonful of freshly made tea.

Boil the rest of the sugar and water for one minute and when this is cool add to the rest. Cover as directed or fit fermentation lock and leave until all fermentation has ceased.

BRAVERY'S OWN SCOTCH

This is another recipe that has become well known amongst wine makers throughout the country.

1½ lb. wheat, 1½ lb. raisins, 4 oranges, 3½ lb. sugar, 1 oz.

yeast, 9 *pts water and* 1 *tablespoonful of freshly made strong tea.*

Prepare the wheat and raisins as already advised and put them in the fermenting vessel with the sliced oranges and their peel.

Boil half the sugar in three quarts of water for two minutes and pour this over the material in the fermenting vessel. Mix well and when cool add the yeast. Cover as directed and ferment for seven days, stirring well each day and covering again at once. Strain and wring out dry and put the strained liquor into a gallon jar with the tea. Then boil the rest of the sugar in the remaining three pints of water for two minutes and when cool add to the rest.

Cover again as directed or fit fermentation lock and leave until all fermentation has ceased.

RAISIN WINE

3 *lb. raisins*, 3 *lemons*, 2 *lb. sugar*, 9 *pts water*, 1 *oz. yeast*, 1 *tablespoonful of freshly made tea.*

Less sugar than usual is required here because the large amount of raisins will give a lot of sugar to the wine—which will not be dry. For a dry raisin wine use only one and a quarter pounds of sugar.

Put the raisins with the sliced lemons and the tea in the fermenting vessel. Boil all the sugar in all the water (or half the water at a time if your saucepan is on the small side), and add to the rest while boiling. When cool, add the yeast and ferment for fourteen days, stirring daily and covering again at once.

Strain and wring out as dry as you can and put the strained

liquor into a gallon jar. Cover as directed or fit fermentation lock and leave until all fermentation has ceased.

PRUNE PORT

6 lb. prunes, 2 lemons, 3½ lb. sugar, 9 pts water, 1 oz. yeast. (No tea in this one.)

Wash the prunes in water in which one Campden tablet has been dissolved and put them in the fermenting vessel.

Boil two pounds sugar in seven pints water and pour over the fruit while boiling. Allow to cool and add the yeast. Cover and ferment for ten days, crushing well each day as soon as the fruit has become soft.

After ten days, crush well and strain out the solids. Wring out as dry as you can and put the strained liquor in a gallon jar.

Boil the rest of the sugar in the remaining two pints of water and when cool add to the rest. Cover as directed or fit fermentation lock and leave until all fermentation has ceased.

CURRANT WINE

No lemons are required here as currants contain sufficient acid, neither is tea required.

4 lb. currants, 1 lb. raisins, 2¾ lb. sugar, 1 oz. yeast, 9 pts water.

Prepare the currants by the method given for prunes in the previous recipe, and put them in the fermenting vessel.

Boil half the sugar (or roughly half) in seven pints water

for two minutes and pour on to the currants at once. Allow to cool and add the yeast.

Cover as directed and ferment for twelve days, crushing and covering again each day.

After twelve days, strain out the solids and wring out as dry as you can and put the strained liquor into a gallon jar.

Boil the rest of the sugar in the remaining two pints of water for two minutes and when cool add to the rest. Cover as directed or fit fermentation lock and leave until all fermentation has ceased.

DRIED APRICOT WINE

This is a really delightful pale gold wine that most people like as a dry wine. See 'Low-Alcohol Wines for the Ladies', page 80.

6 lb. dried apricots, 2 oranges, 3½ lb. sugar, 9 pts water, 1 oz. yeast, 1 tablespoonful of freshly made tea.

Put the apricots in the fermenting vessel with the cut-up oranges and their peel. Fold the orange peel and squeeze to get as much oil out of it as you can.

Boil two pounds sugar in seven pints water for two minutes and pour over the fruits while still boiling. Allow to cool and add the yeast.

Cover as directed and ferment for ten days, crushing by hand each day and covering again at once.

After ten days, strain and wring out as dry as you can and put the strained liquor in the gallon jar. Boil the remaining sugar in the last two pints of water for two minutes and when cool add to the rest, and then add the tea.

Cover as directed or fit fermentation lock and leave until all fermentation has ceased.

DATE WINE

This wine has very little flavour of its own, therefore lemons and oranges must be added to give a nice flavour, and the amount of oranges here will make it into a lovely wine.

However, if you want a wine of little flavour for some special purpose, say, for blending with one that has too much flavour or for flavouring as you wish with an extract or whatever you may have in mind, use no oranges at all.

3 lb. of packeted or loose dates, 2 lemons, 6 oranges (see note), 2 lb. sugar, 9 pts water, 1 oz. yeast, 1 tablespoonful of freshly made tea.

The method of preparing ingredients and for making this wine is identical to that given in the recipe for making dried apricot wine.

PRUNE AND RAISIN VINTAGE

3 lb. prunes, 1 lb. raisins, 1 lb. wheat, 2 lemons, 2 oranges, 3 lb. sugar, 9 pts water, 1 oz. yeast.

Prepare the raisins, prunes and wheat as has already been advised and put them with the sliced oranges and lemons in the fermenting vessel.

Boil half the sugar in seven pints water for two minutes and pour over the ingredients while still boiling. Allow to cool and add the yeast.

Cover as directed and ferment the mixture for ten days,

crushing well each day and stirring up the wheat and covering again at once.

After ten days, strain out the solids, and wring out as dry as you can and put the strained liquor in a gallon jar.

Boil the rest of the sugar in the remaining two pints water and when cool add to the rest. Cover as directed or fit fermentation lock and leave until all fermentation has ceased.

IRISH WHISKEY

2 lb. wheat, 1 lb. raisins, 1 lb. potatoes, 2 lemons, 4 oranges, 1 oz yeast, 3 lb. sugar, 9 pts water.

Prepare the wheat and raisins as has already been directed and put them in the fermenting vessel with the sliced lemons and oranges.

Scrub, grate and boil the potatoes in five pints of water for not more than ten minutes, taking off all scum that rises. Boil gently for a little longer if scum still rises at the end of ten minutes until no more scum rises—taking off every bit of it.

Strain this hot liquid over the ingredients in the fermenting vessel and throw the potatoes away. Then boil half the sugar in two pints of water for two minutes and add this to the rest. Allow to cool, add the yeast and ferment the mixture for ten days covered as directed.

After ten days, strain and wring out dry and put the strained liquor into a gallon jar. Boil the rest of the sugar in the remaining two pints of water and when cool add this to the rest. Cover as directed or fit fermentation lock and leave until all fermentation has ceased.

Note

Imaginative readers will be quick to notice that varied amounts of ingredients make very different types of wines and they may wonder whether they can invent a recipe to suit themselves. They can. Almost any recipe in this chapter may be varied to suit individual tastes, or it may be modified and other ingredients or flavourings added. Take care when altering recipes not to use too much of any particular kind so that your overall amount of ingredients would exceed six pounds, otherwise the wine will be spoiled.

CHAPTER TWELVE

Wines from grapes

In the ordinary way, recipes for wines made entirely from grapes are not a practicable proposition. This is because grapes are merely crushed and fermented without either sugar or water being added. Provided you have enough grapes, making wines from them is the simplest wine-making of all—that is, of course, provided you have good-quality grapes, all ripe and on the sweet side.

Any variety or colour make good wine, including small outdoor-grown grapes—again, provided they are fully ripe. Small unpruned bunches often contain a lot of small undeveloped fruits between the large juicy ones and these must be removed before the bunches are crushed. The whole bunches, stalks as well, are used as these add something to the wine.

The yeast forming the bloom on your grapes may be the kind that will make excellent wines, but we cannot be sure of this owing to the near-certainty that wild yeast and bacteria are present with it. As we have seen in previous chapters, we must destroy these yeasts and bacteria and add yeasts of our choice to make the wine for us.

You will need at least twenty pounds of grapes to be assured of a gallon of wine—and this amount may not make one gallon of wine, though it may make one gallon of strained 'must'. Therefore the more grapes you have the better.

If enough grapes are available, the process is as follows.

Method

Put all the grapes in a suitable vessel and crush them,

making sure each grape is crushed. Measure as near as you can or judge as accurately as possible the amount of pulp you have and to each gallon allow one Campden tablet or four grains sodium metabisulphite. Dissolve this in an egg-cupful of warm water and stir into the pulp and leave for twenty-four hours.

After this, give the mixture a thorough mixing and churning and then add the yeast. The mixture should then be left to ferment for five days.

Following this, the pulp should be strained through a strong coarse cloth to prevent bursting and wrung out as dry as you can. The liquor should then be put into jars and fermented in the same way as other wines.

A good plan when doing this is to mix a quart of water with the grape pulp and to crush this well to get as much from the skins and the pulp as you can. If you do this, you must add one pound of sugar and dissolve it by warming the juice just enough for this purpose. This thinner juice may be mixed with the rest but *before* the better-quality juice is put into jars.

Where grapes only are used with no water (as suggested above) it must be borne in mind that to get enough alcohol for a stable wine we must have between two and two and a half pounds of sugar to the gallon. Juice crushed from grapes rarely contains this much, therefore it would be wise to add one pound when the fruit is crushed and before the juice is put into jars. If the wine turns out dry, it may be sweetened. We may use a hydrometer to find the sugar content so that we know how much to add to give the amount of alcohol we need, but this is not for beginners without previous experience in this sort of thing. The better plan is to follow my suggestions above, and if the wine is dry to sweeten it and then preserve it with

Campden tablets or metabisulphite as directed in chapter six.

Since the colour comes from the skins, if we want a red wine from black grapes we ferment the skins as directed earlier in this chapter. A white wine from black grapes is made by crushing the grapes and pressing out the juice and fermenting the juice only. The difference in the process already described is that instead of fermenting the skins for five days, the juice is pressed out after it has been allowed to soak for twenty-four hours.

If you happen to be making some other fruit wine such as elderberry, plum, blackberry or damson, at the same time as making grape wine, it would be a good idea to put the strained fruit pulp which would otherwise be discarded into the 'must' of the other fruit and let it ferment there. But do not alter the fermentation times of the other recipe that you are using for the other fruit.

If an abundance of grapes is not available the following recipes will be found especially valuable. The methods to use are those given for making the various fresh fruit wines in chapter two. Bear in mind that the grapes must be fermented when a red wine is required whilst the juice only is fermented when a white wine is required. This applies to black grapes, of course; you can do anything you like with those called amber or the green ones.

Recipe 1
9 *to* 12 *lb. grapes,* 2 *lb. raisins,* 2 *qts water,* – *lb. sugar, port yeast or burgundy yeast.*

Recipe 2
8 *to* 10 *lb. grapes,* 2 *lb. prunes,* 2 *qts water,* 2 *lb. sugar, port yeast or burgundy yeast.*

Recipe 3
10 *lb. black grapes,* 1 *lb. prunes,* 2 *lb. raisins,* 1½ *lb. sugar,* 4 *pts water, port or burgundy yeast.*

Recipe 4
10 *lb. grapes,* 2 *lb. elderberries,* 4 *pts water,* 2 *lb. sugar, port yeast or burgundy yeast.*

Recipe 5
8 *lb.* grapes, 6 lb. *damsons or red plums,* 2 *lb. sugar,* 2 *qts water, port or burgundy yeast.*

Note

Owing to the difficulty in getting the juice from plums and damsons, the pulp must be fermented for a time, so it is not practicable to ferment the juice only in this recipe.

Recipe 6
8 *to* 10 *lb. grapes,* 2 *lb. blackberries,* 4 *pts water, port or burgundy yeast,* 2 *lb. sugar.*

Note

Nutrient is not needed because the grape juice provides sufficient.

CHAPTER THIRTEEN

Liqueurs

IN my grandmother's day brandy cost about five shillings a bottle (now we know what is meant by 'the good old days') and her recipes call for gallons of the stuff as casually as today's call for one measly bottle.

Nevertheless, one bottle of gin, whisky or brandy will give two bottles of the finished product with a high percentage of alcohol at half the cost of the commercial product.

Before going on to the recipes, let me explain that a home-made wine usually has an alcohol content of fourteen per cent by volume (approximately 24° proof). Such a wine will keep well because this amount of alcohol is usually high enough to destroy souring yeast and the bacteria which cause vinegariness immediately it comes into contact with them. Thus it will be seen that a nice percentage of alcohol acts as its own preservative.

The alcohol content of commercial wines rarely exceeds twenty per cent by volume (approximately 35° proof); more often they range between fourteen per cent by volume (approximately 24° proof) and nineteeen per cent by volume (approximately 33° proof), which is a high percentage of alcohol. Clearly, then, we could very well dilute the 70° proof of gin (forty per cent by volume) to 35° proof (twenty per cent by volume) by making one bottle into two bottles and still have a very strong sloe gin.

Whisky and rum could be similarly treated, while brandy might well be diluted even more owing to its higher spirit content. Bear in mind that it would be unwise to reduce the proof to below 30°. The best plan to start with is to make one bottle into two as the recipes advise or make half a bottle into a whole bottle by using half of everything in the recipes.

You could make three or four bottles from one bottle of the spirit if you were proposing to use it up fairly quickly, such as at a party or over the three-day Christmas.

Naturally, we shall be diluting the flavours of the spirits we are using, but we shall be adding the flavours of our choice to counter-balance this. In any case, the commercial spirits mentioned above are rarely drunk neat. Whisky is usually diluted with water (which in my opinion is nigh on a crime) or ginger or soda, while rum is often diluted with peppermint or orange cordial. Gin is usually diluted with lemon or orange cordial to make the popular gin and orange, etc. And in most cases the spirit is diluted to one-third of its volume. Therefore, the proof spirit content of the whisky and soda or gin and orange served over the bar has been reduced to about 23° proof. The sloe gin we shall be making with these recipes will be 35° proof while the cherry brandy will be 40° proof. Bear this in mind while drinking them otherwise you will finish up under the table in double-quick time.

If you happen to have some home-made sloe wine, damson wine, orange wine, cherry wine or some other sort of home-made wine, you may employ one bottle of the spirits mentioned to make more than two bottles of cherry brandy, sloe gin or whichever you have in mind. This point is covered fully further on in this chapter.

The following recipes produce wines which are neither sweet nor dry; if you like a slightly sweet wine increase the amount of sugar by half that given in the recipes. On the other hand, if you like wines drier than average reduce the amount of sugar by half.

In the recipes called liqueurs, the amount of sugar should remain as in the recipes.

Note

As we shall be using bottles as our means of measuring our materials, bear in mind that a bottle is a bottle and that half a bottle is half a bottle. A bottle—the recognized standard wine bottle or the bottles containing spirits—hold five gills; this is one gill more than a pint. Many bottles containing imported wines hold one pint. Because we shall be making exactly two bottles from one bottle of the spirit we are using, be sure that the second bottle you use holds the same amount as the bottle of spirit you are using. If you are using White Horse whisky or Booth's gin, try to use a similar second bottle.

CHERRY BRANDY LIQUEUR

$1\frac{1}{2}$ lb. black cherries, 8 oz. white sugar, 1 bottle brandy, 8 blanched almonds (these are usually added, but personal tastes must decide).

Wash the cherries and let them drain. Pour the brandy into a four-pound Kilner jar (these are best), then stone and halve the cherries carefully and add them to the brandy. Add the almonds if you like them.

Screw down tightly and put in a cool, preferably dark, place for six to eight weeks. Give the jar a good shaking twice a week.

Strain and squeeze and put the liquid into a smaller jar and then put away as before and leave to clear. Then pour or siphon into two wine bottles—putting exactly half into each. Then boil the sugar in one pint of water for two minutes. When this is cool, fill the bottles to within one inch of where the cork will reach. Shake well to ensure thorough mixing. Seal and keep for one month.

DAMSON GIN

1 *lb. damsons*, 3 *oz. sugar*, 1 *bottle gin*.

Wash, dry, stone and halve the damsons carefully and put them in a four-pound Kilner jar. Sprinkle the sugar over them and then pour in the gin.

Screw down tightly and leave in a cool dark place for three months (or two months if you are in a hurry to use the product), giving a good shaking once or twice a week.

Strain and squeeze and put the strained damson gin into a smaller jar, screw down again and put it away to clear. Then pour carefully (or siphon) the clear gin off the deposit putting exactly half into two bottles. Then fill the bottles to within one inch of where the corks will reach with boiled water that has cooled naturally. Cork hard, seal and keep for one month.

SLOE GIN

1 *lb. sloes*, 5 *oz. sugar*, 1 *bottle gin*.

Wash the sloes and let them drain.

Prick the sloes all over with a silver, or stainless-steel, fork or large darning needle and put them in a four-pound Kilner jar. Sprinkle the sugar over them and then pour in the gin.

Screw down tightly and put in a cool dark place for six weeks. Give the jar a good shaking once a week.

Strain and squeeze and put the strained sloe gin into a smaller jar, screw down tightly again and put away until clear.

Pour carefully (or siphon) the clear sloe gin off the deposit and put exactly half into each of two bottles. Fill the bottles to within one inch of where the corks will reach with boiled water that has cooled naturally.

Mix well by shaking, cork, seal and keep for one month.

ORANGE WHISKY

4 *oranges*, 2 *lemons*, 2 *Seville oranges* (*or an extra ordinary orange and lemon*), 4 *oz. sugar*, 1 *bottle whisky*.

Peel the fruits and remove all the white pith. Crush well and put the pulp in a four-pound Kilner jar. Grate the rind of one orange (not a Seville), avoiding any white pith, and add this to the pulp. Sprinkle in the sugar and pour on the whisky. Screw down tightly and put the jar in a cool dark place for a week—giving it a shake every day.

Strain into another jar and squeeze and screw down again tightly. Then put it away to clear.

Pour or siphon the clear whisky into bottles, putting exactly half into each. Then fill the bottles to within an inch of where the corks will reach with boiled water that has cooled naturally.

Cork hard, seal and keep for at least two months.

ORANGE GIN

6 *oranges*, 1 *lemon*, 2 *Seville oranges* (*or an extra ordinary orange and lemon*), 5 *oz. sugar*, 1 *bottle gin*.

Proceed as for orange whisky.

FRUIT LIQUEURS

There is no need to give separate recipes for each fruit because the same process may be used for all suitable fresh fruit of your choice. The following lists the most suitable fruits for liqueur-making and the amounts given usually produce sufficient flavour—though not enough juice—to make two bottles of liqueur when using one bottle of brandy. If not enough juice is produced from the amounts of fruit given, make up to the amount required with boiled water, bearing in mind that half a pound of sugar occupies the space of a quarter-pint while one pound occupies half a pint space and so on.

All these liqueurs will have a spirit content of 40° proof—which, as we have seen, is a high spirit content.

As we shall be using a spirit of 80° proof, we could make two and a half bottles by using a little more juice, a little more water and an ounce or two more sugar and still have a product of 32° proof—which is a nice spirit content.

If at party time economy is essential, three or even four bottles of a liqueur-type wine could be made from one bottle of brandy or, say, cherry brandy, sloe gin or whatever you have in mind, if it were intended to use them up over a weekend or over a three-day Christmas. See 'Making Liqueurs from wines', page 127, and 'Making Liqueurs from Extracts', page 122.

One bottle of liqueur may be made by using exactly half the amounts listed below and a little water.

Fresh fruit	Quantity lb.	Sugar oz.	Brandy
Blackcurrants	1	4	1 bottle
Redcurrants	1½	5	,,
Strawberries	1½	3	,,
Cherries	2	4	,,
Raspberries	1	5	,,
Loganberries	1	4	,,
Blackberries	1	5	,,

Crush the fruit by hand, put in a basin and keep in a very warm place for twelve hours, well covered. Strain carefully through several thicknesses of fine muslin or other suitable material. Allow to drain rather than squeeze.

Put the strained juice into a bottle of the same size as the brandy bottle and fill with boiled water that has been allowed to cool. Mix well by shaking, cork hard and put in a cool place for one hour. By this time a deposit will have formed. Pour the clear juice off this deposit, leaving a little juice rather than allowing any deposit through. The deposit may cause permanent cloudiness if boiled with the clear juice.

Put the clear juice in a small unchipped enamel saucepan with the sugar and boil gently for two minutes. When cool put exactly half into two bottles of the same size as the brandy bottle and then fill up with brandy. Add a few drops of boiled water if the liquid does not reach to within one inch of where the corks will reach. Then cork hard and seal after giving a good shaking to ensure thorough mixing and keep for a month at least. If a film of deposit forms at the bottom of the bottles, decant before serving.

LIQUEURS FROM EXTRACTS

This field of liqueur-making is the most modern and simplest, and I am proud to be the first to offer details of it in a book. All that has hitherto been heard of this method of making liqueurs has been in the form of unadvertised leaflets. It was through one of these leaflets that I stumbled on to what I believe to be one of the greatest boons ever to come the way of ordinary people. True, one needs a bottle of brandy or gin or some other spirit to start with, but as Christmas begins to come along or at party times at any time of the year, reckoning the cost of the drinks bill is always a headache; economy is often essential. Economy frequently means being satisfied with inferior products, but this is now unnecessary. Top-quality products at half the price of commercial products are within the reach of everybody.

The trials I have carried out with these extracts both for making liqueurs and wines have proved one hundred per cent successful—if they had not, I would not be passing on details to my readers. I do not publish a recipe until it has been tested several times by myself.

The following are amongst the many extracts known as T'Noirot Extracts. I have added a description to the first four to give you an idea of their value and also an idea of what they are actually made. All are scientifically blended for the purpose for which they are designed and are not in any way synthetic. They do not contain substitutes for the genuine ingredients.

Red Curaçao

Distillation and macaration of orange zests and green bigarade, caramel.

Kümmel

Distillation of caraway seeds, aniseed, mint leaves and peel of citrons.

Cherry Brandy

Extracts of cherry by distillation and macaration, and hydrolats of fruits.

Ratafia

Ratafia des Quatre Fruits—otherwise extract of mixed fruits.

White Curaçao	*Prunelle*
Mirabelle	*Sloe Gin*
Juniper Gin (commercial gin flavour)	*Yellow Convent*

Green Convent   *White Mint*
Green Mint   *Cream of Apricot*
                                        and others.

Note

The 'mints' above do, incidentally, make very excellent hot drinks for winter time if diluted with hot water at the rate of one bottle of extract to a wine bottle of water in which four ounces of sugar have been dissolved. More sugar may be added to taste and if the flavour is too strong for you when diluted to this extent, dilute even further. I usually make nearly two bottles of hot mint drink from one bottle of extract.

To begin with, most of you will plump for extracts whose flavours you are familiar with—sloe gin, cherry brandy and juniper gin. But whichever your choice, the method is the same with all. The extracts cost about two shillings or two and six a bottle and are obtainable from dealers in Home Wine-Makers equipment.

Directions on the bottles of extracts are for making one bottle of cherry brandy (or whichever you choose), from one bottle of the extract and a bottle of brandy (or gin, according to which you are making), and if you want to follow these directions, all very well.

But I fancy that the cost will deter many of you from doing this. Therefore, I feel that you will prefer the following directions.

As we have already seen in this chapter, gin and whisky of 70° proof (forty per cent by volume) may be diluted to 35° proof (twenty per cent by volume), by making one bottle into two, and still have a high percentage of alcohol.

Brandy may be diluted even more owing to its higher alcohol content. By making one bottle of brandy into two and a half bottles of cherry brandy we shall be diluting to 32° proof which is the alcohol content of the higher-alcohol wines.

One bottle of gin may be made into two bottles of sloe gin while one bottle of whisky may be made into two bottles of Ratafia liqueur or, with whisky, almost any of the extracts may be used.

As these extracts are designed to flavour one bottle of liqueur it might be necessary to use one and a half to two bottles of the extract to flavour the two bottles of the wine that we shall be making from the one bottle of spirit. But much will depend on personal tastes. In the tests I have made with these extracts, I found that when one bottle of extract was mixed with a wine bottle full of sugar water (syrup as described later on) and then mixed with one bottle of spirit, the flavour was just to my liking. If the reader prefers a slightly stronger flavour a little more extract may be added.

Method

Select the extract you propose to use and decide on the spirit of your choice, see 'Suitable Combinations', page 126, and proceed as follows. Put one pint of water and six ounces of sugar together in a small unchipped enamel saucepan. Bring to the boil and cut off the heat at once and add the extract. Leave to cool, but give a stir occasionally.

When cool stir well to keep any deposit distributed and, using a glass or polythene funnel, put exactly half into each of two wine bottles of equal size. Then fill each with the spirit. Add a few drops of boiled water (or a little more extract if you wish), if the level does not rise to within an inch of where the corks will reach. Several of the extracts contain a tiny amount of minute solids so that a slight film of deposit sometimes forms during storage. Pour the clear wine carefully or siphon into fresh bottles before serving. Simple enough. Where two bottles have been made, as above, the alcohol content will be high and the product will keep well if the bottles are sealed and stored on their sides.

Where economy demands more than two bottles of liqueur from one bottle of spirit, certain points must be borne in mind. The main one is that if the percentage of alcohol by volume is reduced to below sixteen (28° proof), there is a risk that the wine will not keep for more than a few days. On the other hand, if the bottles are sterilized along with the corks and the bottles are then sealed and stored on their sides, there is no reason why the wine should not keep well until opened. But once opened it should be used up within a few days.

To give a guide to the limit you could dilute safely and still have a nice percentage of alcohol, the limit would be to make one bottle of spirit into three bottles of wine by using more extract, more sugar and water. Such dilution would give you thirteen per cent of alcohol by volume or 22° proof. This alcohol content is that found in less expensive wines.

SUITABLE COMBINATIONS

Extract	Spirit
Red Curacao	Whisky
Ratafia	Whisky
Cherry Brandy	Brandy
Sloe Gin	Gin (sweetened or unsweetened)
Juniper Gin (commercial flavour)	Gin (sweetened or unsweetened)

Extract	*Spirit*
Cream of Apricot	Brandy
Cream of Peach	Brandy
Cream of Green Mint	Rum or Gin
Cream of White Mint	Rum or Gin

The above extracts and spirits are those usually used together, but there is nothing to prevent you using a combination that you might prefer.

LIQUEURS AND PARTY SPECIALS
FROM HOME-MADE WINES

Most of us have stocks of home-made wines and, at party time or at Christmas, we often wonder how we can turn them into 'party specials' and do so inexpensively. The main question always is: how much spirit to add to get a given percentage of alcohol.

Firstly, and in the ordinary way, a well-made wine will not need doctoring of this sort because if fermentation was satisfactory the alcohol content will be in the region of fourteen or fifteen per cent by volume (24° to 26° proof). This is the alcohol content of most commercial wines; indeed, some are lower in alcohol than this while others are, of course, higher.

Come party time the question is often one of economy— how to make that one bottle of Scotch, or gin or rum, go farther without the economy being noticeable. As already mentioned, spirits are rarely drunk neat; additions of some sort are usually employed, such as ginger, orange or lemon cordial, and these reduce the alcohol content to about a quarter. For those who want to experiment a bit on their own accord, the table on page 128 shows the relation between alcohol by volume and proof spirit, and the range covered by this allows for the limits within which they will be working.

Those not wishing to start from scratch will find the following guidance useful.

Let me begin with whisky, gin or rum of 70° proof.

Wines made with the following fruits are ideal for mixing with gin, either sweetened or unsweetened—damson, sloe, lemon, orange.

We have a bottle of one or the other of these wines and a bottle of gin handy.

The gin contains forty per cent of alcohol by volume and a bottle of wine fourteen per cent. Mix the two and you have (for the sake of simplicity) twice as much of both. Therefore you have twenty per cent by volume (the gin) and seven per cent by volume (the wine), total twenty-seven per cent by volume.

To make it even simpler:

The gin   40 per cent by volume
The wine 14 per cent ,,   ,,

———————

54 per cent

———————

But because the volume (amount) has been doubled, the alcohol content has been reduced by half—twenty seven per cent by volume. As we can get fifty-four per cent of alcohol in this way we could use two bottles of wine and one of gin and get three bottles of a product containing eighteen per cent.

Note

It is important to understand that when two bottles of wine at 14% of alcohol are put together you have twice as much wine still at 14%. But when you do this for the purpose of fortifying, the alcohol in each bottle must be accounted for. Therefore, three bottles of wine each containing 14% equals 42%, plus one bottle of gin at 40% = 82%. Divide this figure by the number of resulting bottles—in this case four bottles—and each will contain just over 20%.

	Going further—5 bottles at 14% =	70%
	One bottle gin at	40%
	total	110%

In this case six bottles result, therefore 110 ÷ 6 = 18% approximately. The same would apply when whisky or rum are used.

Wines more suitable for mixing with whisky are:

Root wines (not beetroot).
Root wines made with cereals such as wheat, and with raisins, or both, or with wheat or raisins alone added.
Grain wines—those made mainly with wheat or maize, etc.
Orange.
Dandelion.

Wines more suitable for mixing with rum:

Root wines with a rather higher than average acid content.
Other more acid wines such as rhubarb.
Orange.
Lemon.
Grapefruit.

Wines more suitable for mixing with port and other high-alcohol red wines:

Elderberry and all other red wines whether made from one fruit or a mixture of fruits, or mixtures of fruits and grains such as wheat or maize.

White wines or the paler-coloured ones made from such fruits as raisins, raspberries, loganberries, red or white currants, etc., may be mixed with the higher-alcohol white 'ports' or high-alcohol white wines.

Note

Owing to the lower alcohol content of port as compared with spirits, the mixing should be confined to one bottle of wine to the bottle of port if they are required for keeping. Two to one mixing may be practised where it is intended to use up the product within, say, three or four days.

LIQUEURS FROM HOME-MADE WINES

Home-made wines make splendid liqueurs.

The usual practice is to use strongly flavoured wines, sugar and whisky or brandy. But there is nothing to prevent you using gin or rum if you prefer.

If the wine you propose to use is sweet use only three ounces of sugar. If it is a medium-sweet, use five ounces. If it is dry, use seven ounces of sugar to one bottle of wine. Warm the wine and dissolve the sugar in it. Be careful not to let the wine become hot or even over-warm. When the sugar has dissolved, pour into a bottle large enough to hold both the sweetened wine and the spirit and mix well together. Then bottle, and you have two bottles of first-class stuff.

Where economy is essential, a half-bottle of brandy or whisky may be used with one bottle of the wines of your choice.

The following table gives the comparisons between alcohol by volume and proof spirit. Bear in mind that it is wisest not to dilute to below sixteen per cent by volume. This does not mean that the diluted product must of necessity 'go off' if kept; indeed, wines as low as fourteen per cent of alcohol by volume keep well, provided the bottles and corks are sterilized before the wine is put into them and the bottles are then sealed and stored on their sides until used. For the best sterilizing solution for our purpose see page 26.

Degrees Proof	Alcohol by Volume per cent
80	46
70	40
61·2	35
52·4	30
43·8	25
35	20
33·1	19
31·4	18
29·7	17
28	16
24·5	14
22·7	13
21·6	12

Do not imagine that a wine or a diluted spirit is low—actually low—in alcohol because the alcohol content has been reduced to fourteen per cent by volume. When we refer to a low-alcohol wine we really mean a wine that is not high in alcohol. A high-alcohol wine is usually in the region of eighteen per cent by volume while the low-alcohol wines are usually in the region of ten per cent or even just below this. Wines lower than fourteen per cent by volume are usually preserved with sulphur dioxide to prevent souring or acetification—vinegariness. From this it will be clear that if you want to dilute to lower than fourteen per cent by volume you may do so provided you are prepared to preserve your products. Preservation is necessary because an alcohol content of below fourteen per cent by volume will not preserve a wine by itself. I have already mentioned that a good percentage of alcohol acts as its own preservative; below fourteen per cent by volume is not —strictly speaking—a good percentage of alcohol. But many people like the lower-alcohol wines more than others; indeed, many imported popular wines are in the region of ten per cent by volume—some are as low as eight per cent by volume. The fact that they keep well is because they are preserved.

Preserving is easily carried out by using Campden fruit-preserving tablets—bottles of twenty tablets are obtainable at all chemists for about tenpence.

Two of these tablets will usually preserve a gallon of wine, though one tablet is often enough for one gallon. Therefore, if you are making half-gallons of the products in this chapter and are making them below fourteen per cent by volume, clearly one tablet will preserve half a gallon while half a tablet will preserve a quart. Note here that a quarter-tablet will be enough if the alcohol content is to remain above ten per cent by volume, but do not reduce to below a quarter-tablet per quart of the product.

Just crush the tablet—or part—with something non-metal, then dissolve the powder in a little of the liquid and then stir into the bulk.

Sterilizing Solution

In the ordinary way, and where the alcohol content of your finished products is to remain above fourteen per cent by volume, thorough cleansing of the bottles and boiling of corks before fitting them is usually enough, but where the alcohol is to be reduced to below fourteen per cent by volume it is wise to sterilize the bottles in the following manner: Crush four Campden fruit-preserving tablets and dissolve the powder in a pint of warm water. Rinse the insides of the already cleaned bottles with this solution and then rinse them out with boiled water that has cooled a bit. All this may seem rather a bother, but it takes only a couple of minutes.

Having filled the bottles to within an inch of where the corks will reach, ram the corks home hard and then seal with sealing wax. Store bottles on their sides.

Note

These precautions are necessary only when it is intended to keep the lower-alcohol products for more than a few days.

CHAPTER FOURTEEN

Some questions and answers

Reclaiming the Yeast

Q. I have been making wines for a number of years and upon your recommendation have recently graduated to using wine yeasts. I find these a little more expensive to use and have hit upon the idea of taking a little of one lot of fermenting wine to 'start off' another batch instead of using a freshly started 'starter bottle'.

This new batch is fermenting well on the yeast taken from the near-finished lot. But I am now worried in case I have been rather an ass instead of a clever dick. Do you think everything will be O.K.?

A. Quite O.K. I often do this myself, but only once. By this I mean that if I take yeast from one lot to ferment another—that is as far as I go. I do not take a little of this second lot to start a third. My reason for this is that I like to bear in mind that all cultivated plant life (wine yeast being cultivated plant life) is subject to reversion to its wild state.

Mind you, I am not suggesting that reversion would of necessity take place, but it could if this practice were carried too far. Though there would be no harm in taking two lots of yeast from the one wine already fermenting to start two separate batches. The danger would come in taking yeast from one to the next, and then to the third and fourth and so on.

134

SLOW FERMENT

Q. When using bakers' yeast, as I have been doing for years, I find that when sampling a fermenting 'must' after fourteen days' fermentation I get a good idea of the kind of wine I can expect when fermentation has ceased altogether, and at this time I have found that most of the sugar has been used up and the wine, while still over-sweet, is not unbearably so. But now that I am using wine yeast, I find that after fourteen days' fermentation the wine is always sweeter than when I used bakers' yeast. This puzzles me, and I am wondering if the yeast is working as well as it should be. I must add, though, that the completely finished wines that I have so far made with wine yeast are better than those I have made with bakers' yeast.

A. The point you are overlooking here is that when using bakers' yeast you usually add about an ounce. But when using wine yeast you are using very little yeast to start with.

Obviously, and because alcohol is the result of yeast reproduction, more alcohol is made in less time and therefore more sugar used up in less time when more yeast is used at the start.

The little bit of yeast you add either in tablet form or as a yeast culture cannot hope to produce so much alcohol in as little time as the quite large amount of bakers' yeast. But given time for reproduction to go on until millions of generations have lived and died in the course of producing the alcohol we want, the result will be the same.

It occurs to me that you might be in a hurry to get fermentation over in quick time, and you might like to try an experiment. But do not blame me if this is not one hundred per cent successful—though I can find no reason for it not being just that.

Now, we know that bakers' yeast will produce about fourteen per cent of alcohol by volume in quite a short time. We also know that wine yeast makes about seventeen to eighteen per cent of alcohol by volume. Why not use bakers' yeast to get that initial fourteen per cent in a short time and, as fermentation nears completion, add your wine yeast to make that extra three or four per cent? In this way you should get eighteen per cent in far less time.

I must repeat that this is only a suggestion, and I shall be trying this idea out for myself later on; until then I cannot promise one hundred per cent success.

Too Much Froth

Q. I am using a nutrient that causes a lot of frothing at the time of adding it. Sometimes this froths over the tops of the jars and, when it subsides, a lot of this froth smothers the inside of the top quarter of the jar. I don't want to change my nutrient because it has proved itself a good one. Would you say it might be a good idea to add the total amount in three separate lots? One lot when the 'must' is first prepared, the second when I add the first lot of sugar and the third lot when I add the second lot of sugar; this stage is, of course, the final stage. And does it matter if I leave that unsightly froth clinging to the inside of the jar until I next transfer to another jar or, in the final stage, would any harm come in leaving the froth where it is until all fermentation has ceased?

A. Let me deal with the last part of your query first. The froth that is bothering you is part nutrient, part yeast. Ignore its presence. Carry on as if it were not there at all—though I will admit that it does look unsightly. It is no bother to clean out of the jar when it becomes empty and it does no harm while remaining in the fermenting wine.

Some of this may break away and come over when the wine is being transferred to another jar, but it will settle in the form of lees later on and will be left behind at racking time.

As for adding the nutrient in stages, this is a good idea if you are using a gallon jar for making a gallon of wine. If you have jars that hold a good deal more than one gallon and make only a gallon at a time in them, all the nutrient may be added at once.

Bear in mind that when you know and understand the rules of successful wine-making, any idea of your own provided it does not go against the rules will work out all right.

VIGOROUS FERMENT

Q. I was about to set about transferring my fermenting wine to another jar in order to add more sugar-water, this being after fourteen days' fermentation; but I found the ferment so vigorous that I felt it best to leave it for another week. This meant that the ferment was still very vigorous when the next lot of sugar was due to be added, so I left this second addition for a further week also. Your instructions seem emphatic about fermentation times and I am now worrying in case I should have adhered strictly to your rules.

A. Stop worrying. It is the common-sense approach such as yours that turns out good wines and good wine-makers. My directions are nothing more, really, that a general plan of action to be followed under ordinary circumstances. Those following them will make good wines, but it does not mean that they have to stick to everything I tell them. As I have written elsewhere, learn the simple rules and success follows naturally. When you know and understand the rules, you know how many you may break safely and how you may alter recipes and directions according to your own wishes and circumstances.

FERMENTATION LOCK PUZZLE

Q. All the following incidents occurred in a single week and I am puzzled as to what has happened and what I ought to do.

Firstly, when fitting the lock to a jar of wine that was rather warm the lock began working in reverse. But later on I found that this was working normally. Then, later still, I found that while the wine was fermenting, the water in the lock remained level. Then, later still, the water was pushed up on the wrong side of the lock as if a bubble was going to pass through in the wrong direction—e.g. into the jar.

A. All very puzzling to the beginner, but all very natural. I have these little tricks played on myself sometimes and this is what has happened in your case.

Firstly, the lock would work in reverse if the wine happened to be on the very warm side when put into the jar because this would drive out the air—or most of it—so that when the wine cooled, air was drawn back into the jar. This is evident because the lock began to work properly later on when the proper amount of air had been drawn in and when gas from the ferment had begun to create pressure. It is for this reason, and because a rapid drop in temperature will sometimes slow down fermentation and cause the same thing to happen, that it is best to put a little of the sterilizing solution into the lock instead of water. Air passing into the jar through the metabisulphite solution is purified instantly.

Secondly, the water in the lock remained level because you must have had a leak in the wax or in the bung—or somewhere—allowing the gas to escape. If you had twisted the jar so that more than normal bubbles rose you would have found that the lock would begin to work and then stop and the water return to normal in a matter of minutes. This would be caused by a lot of gas pressure not being able to escape from a tiny escape hole so that the lock had to work for a little while. But when the excess gas had escaped and the vigorousness of the ferment caused by twisting the jar had died down, the water would return to normal owing to the leak. Run a warm poker or some other tool round the wax joins, but before you do so make sure the bung is pushed in as tightly as it should be.

The fact that later on the water was pushed up on the wrong side of the lock was most likely owing to a rapid drop in temperature. You did not say whether later still you found the lock to be working again normally, so I presume that you did.

Clearly, from these questions and answers, it will be evident that the beginner should use glass jars in preference to stone ones so that they can see whether the wine is working or not and then judge whether the lock is behaving itself or not.

Re-Fermentation

Q. As I broke the plastic seal on a bottle of last year's elderberry wine, the cork shot through the open skylight of the outhouse and half the wine followed it in one almighty gush. I opened the last six bottles of the same batch and the corks flew—but not so badly. The wine fizzed up to the tops of the bottles but did not overflow.

Deciding it best to put the lot into a gallon jar and to fit a lock, I now find that this is working quite fast.

Do you think the wine will be all right and did I do the right thing in putting it under a lock? Further, what could have caused this bottle to ferment, obviously not bacteria because the wine tastes really nice except for the unwanted effervescence?

A. Your elderberry wine has probably suffered the same fate as some other wines that ferment into the winter months where extra warmth during this time is not provided. What has happened is that as fermentation neared completion an especially cold night brought the temperature down and fermentation ceased a little prematurely.

This means that not enough alcohol was made. If enough alcohol *had* been made, any yeast left in the wine would have been dead yeast because the amount of alcohol would have killed it. Clearly the wine has been prevented from fermenting owing to cold, but now that the weather has turned warm the yeast has become active and is going all out to produce all the alcohol that it can.

Leave as it is at present and regard it for all intents and purposes as a new batch of wine. Let it ferment right out and when it has cleared again, bottle it as before.

STEWED FRUIT FLAVOUR

Q. The old methods of making wines that I have been following always advised boiling the fruit. I admit that I rarely had a clear wine to drink, but I did like the flavour of stewed fruit that was given to the wine.

The wines made with the recipes and directions that you sent me over a year ago are lovely wines, brilliantly clear, and everybody likes them more than I do—but only because I prefer that stewed fruit flavour in my wines. Can you tell me how to get this and at the same time get a clear wine? I understand that boiling the fruit is the cause of cloudy wines.

A. You are quite right in assuming that boiling fruits is the cause of cloudy wine. If you want that stewed fruit flavour and a clear wine, you will have to alter the whole process of making wine, but this is quite a simple matter. Any of the recipes I sent you (and for that matter, any fresh fruit wine recipe in this book) may be adapted to give the flavour required.

The method is as follows.

Having crushed the fruit and having added the first lot of water and the Campden tablet, leave the mixture to soak for twenty-four hours. Then squeeze as much as you can and strain the fruit through fine muslin, wringing out all the juice you can get. Then put this juice through a jelly-bag or flannel so that every particle of pectin-bearing fruit is strained out. This may take a long time, but put where it will not be in the way and let it drain without squeezing. Then, when you have all the juice that will run, it may be boiled for a few minutes (say not more than five minutes) to get the flavour you are after. The first lot of sugar would be added to this hot juice and the process thereafter would be the same as given in the methods on pages 38–40, merely adding the sugar and water in stages—either in two stages or in one, as suits you best.

IMPATIENT WINE-MAKER

Q. Not being a patient person and one who is always in the greatest rush when doing anything, I wonder if I may make my wine in two stages instead of the three you advise in various magazines. The wines I have made by following these methods are top rate, but it is just that I have so little time to put to the hobby.

A. If you are, as you say you are, rushed for time, you may do as you wish and add the sugar and water in two stages instead of three. As I have already mentioned, it is common-sense approaches that make good wine makers. My directions are for the very best results, but there is nothing to prevent you altering them slightly to suit your personal circumstances.

Accidental Champagne

Q. On opening a gallon jar of my wine, the lot fizzed up as if it were working vigorously. The deposit in the jar rose up, clouding the wine. This has stopped now and the wine is beginning to clear again. The jar is being left plugged with cotton wool as I am afraid to cork it in case something is wrong. Incidentally, I sampled a drop of this and it is really delightful. Would you please tell me what has happened.

A. Clearly what happened in your case is that you thought fermentation had ceased altogether and bunged down the jar. But a little fermentation went on unnoticed so that you did, in effect, produce by accident a semi-champagne. It is a wonder the bung didn't blow out of the jar.

All you need do now is to leave the wine bunged tightly until the deposit has settled again and then bottle. This will not happen again because the compressed carbon-dioxide gas that caused the effervescence has escaped.

SEDIMENT ON TOP OF WINE

Q. When I put my wine into a jar all the yeast, rose to the top, and because I used two half-gallon jars instead of a gallon jar, the yeast clings to the neck of the bottle and will not sink. Can I do anything about this?

A. Best to leave things as they are for the present. This has been caused through disturbing a vigorous ferment and as soon as this dies down the yeast will settle and no harm will have been done. The same thing happens sometimes with small particles of undissolved isinglass and if you meet this trouble while jars are full, insert a funnel, pour in a little wine or sugar-water and overflow the solids out of the jar.

CHAPTER FIFTEEN

Using the right glass

IT is not so much a matter of using the *right* glass as it is of using the most suitable one. I am at a loss to understand the reason for so many shapes and sizes, which range from a pudding basin on a short stem to a saucer on a single stilt. Who designs them and who the devil buys them? Surely not the people who will be using them. I rather fancy that designers of glasses design them for a certain type of woman, knowing that if they design something elaborate and quite useless it will sell. This need not reflect upon my lady readers because if they are making wines or if wine is being made in their homes, they are too down to earth to have their fancies titillated by something stupidly incongruous. Rather, they will be interested to learn how to serve their wine in a manner that will do it justice, while at the same time enhancing its beauty.

Decorated glasses in a variety of shapes serve no real purpose other than to look nice in the glass cabinet; here we need concern ourselves with one type of glass which is suitable for almost all wines. The glass shown in Figure 3 will disappoint most people, yet it is the best glass to use.

Choose a thin glass so that if you want to warm the wine the palms of your hands will do this readily enough. The stem is there for you to hold in case you want the wine to remain cool. The bowl-shape, curving slightly inwards towards the lip, enables the bouquet to collect for your enjoyment. The thin clear glass enables you to enjoy the colours of the wine, and you'll be surprised how many there are in each wine if you care to look for them.

144

It is essential that glasses be dry, spotlessly clean and brightly polished before use. And equally important is that they be filled to a suitable level.

It is surprising how many people fear being dubbed a

Figure 3. The ideal wine glass showing the correct levels to which different types of wines should be filled.

miser if they do not fill a glass so that the slightest movement results in a stained suit or ruined dress. A glass three parts full is usually too full—see sketch on this page. Remember that you are serving *your* wines, wines that you have taken pride and pains to produce; then why not serve them in a manner that will do them justice?

The best way to drink it

It is surprising that few people know how to get the best from the wine they have made. Too many are content to 'knock it back' without further ado, while others sip and murmur their appreciation.

Few, very few indeed, ever think of taking a biscuit or a bit of bread and cheese with it. Yet the combination of unsweetened biscuit or cream cracker with a few sips of wine is something you are not likely to forget for a long time, and which will become a regular habit once you have tried. I cannot explain the reason, but I assure you that the best wine is superb this way and even a poor wine greatly improved. Try it, and see for yourself.

Appendix

Supplies and yeast mentioned in this book may be obtained from:

Berg & Sons, 511 Puyallup Avenue, Tacoma 2, Wash.

Aetna Bottle Co., 708 Rainier Ave. South, Seattle 44, Wash.

Milan Laboratory, 57 Spring Street, New York, N.Y.

Semplex, Box 7208, Minneapolis, Minn. 55412

Wine Art, P.O. Box 2701, Vancouver 3, B.C., Canada

Suggestions for readers who have difficulty obtaining some of the supplies mentioned in this book.

INVERT SUGAR—This can be made at home by the reader if he has difficulty obtaining same: Put 8 lbs. of ordinary household sugar (white sugar) in a suitable pan with 2 pints of water and ½ ounce of citric acid (obtainable in drugstores), or use the juice of four lemons. Bring slowly to a boil, stirring all the time so that all sugar dissolves. When all sugar is dissolved, allow to boil for half an hour *very gently* without stirring—or stirring only occasionally. Allow this to cool somewhat and then make up to exactly 1 gallon by adding boiled water. You now have INVERT SUGAR— the inversion being caused by the acid. To measure, use 1 pint to each 1 lb. of sugar called for in the recipe—1 pint is equal to 1 lb. of sugar. Store in suitable jars, tightly corked.

YEAST NUTRIENTS—These are blends of chemicals which stimulate yeast reproduction, thereby helping the yeast to make as much alcohol as it is capable of making. There are no actual substitutes, so it is best to obtain them from *Aetna Bottle Co.,* or *Wine Art,* above.

CAMPDEN TABLETS—A substitute is given in the book. Four grains of sodium metabisulphite is equivalent to one Campden tablet. Your druggist will probably think four grains too small an order, so ask him for an order of, say, ten packs of four grains each, and use one four-grain pack for each Campden tablet called for in the recipe. Do *not* buy by the ounce and try to measure four grains yourself.

T' NOIROT EXTRACTS—Stocked by *Aetna Bottle Co.,* Seattle, and by *Wine Art,* Vancouver.

RIBENA—If you cannot obtain this, try to substitute black-currant syrup instead. However, it is best to use RIBENA proper.

CONTAINERS—Good quality tin or stainless steel containers may be used quite safely, but do not use vessels specifically not recommended by the author, and do not use galvanized containers. See page 14.

Note: *Although the liquid measurements given in this book are British, substituting U.S. measurements will in no way affect the quality of the recipes.*

Index

(recipes are indicated by bold type)

HOME BREWING

Without Failures

❦ ⟫✦⟪ ❦

H. E. BRAVERY

Written by the famous author of *Successful Wine Making at Home* (Arc), here is a step-by-step, fool-proof guide to making all types of beer, ale, stout, cider and mead. Mr. Bravery shows how anyone, with the help of a few simple utensils, can make enough beer in an hour's time to last for about two weeks. You learn how commercial brewers prepare their products and suggestions are given on how you may best follow their guidance to obtain results that are often superior to commercially available beverages. Tried and true recipes are included for making beer with malt extracts and grain malts, cider, meads and flower-flavored meads, light mild ale, pale bitter, mild stout, strong stout, light lager, dark beer, brown ale, pale ale, hop beer, etc. All questions of fermentation, bottling, temperature, hydrometer, as well as all necessary utensils are fully taken up.

Illustrated; 4¼" x 7⅛"; 160 pages

cloth: $4.50
paper: 95¢

Books on Health and Nutrition

VITAMIN E
Your Key to a Healthy Heart
Herbert Bailey

WHY IS VITAMIN E therapy for mankind's foremost killing disease still controversial in the United States? This is one of the questions asked and answered in this slashing, fully-documented book. It tells how the efficacy of vitamin E in the treatment of cardiovascular disease was discovered by Dr. Evan Shute of Canada, and of the remarkable cures effected by him and his brother, also a doctor . . . how the author himself suffered a severe heart attack and how in a short time he was restored to normal active life by massive doses of the vitamin . . . how a barrier against vitamin E has been erected in this country by the medical traditionalists of the American Medical Association at the same time that it is being widely used with spectacular results in such medically-advanced countries as England, Germany, France, Italy, and Russia . . . how continuing study indicates that vitamin E may be an effective preventive for diabetes, sterility, arthritis and a variety of other diseases. "Literally worth its weight in gold."
—The Pittsburgh Courier   **$1.65**

GET WELL NATURALLY
Linda Clark

LINDA CLARK believes that relieving human suffering and obtaining optimum health should be mankind's major goal. She insists that it does not matter whether a remedy is orthodox or unorthodox, currently praised or currently scorned in medical circles—as long as it works for you. Miss Clark, who is also the author of **Stay Young Longer,** makes a plea for the natural methods of treating disease—methods which do not rely on either drugs or surgery. Drawing not only from well-known sources but also from folklore and from the more revolutionary modern theories, she presents a wealth of information about diseases ranging from alcoholism to ulcers. Here are frank discussions of such controversial modes of treatment as herbal medicine, auto-therapy, homeopathy, and human electronics, plus some startling facts and theories about nutrition and about the natural ways of treating twenty-two of the most serious illnesses that plague modern man.   **$1.65**

THE LOW-FAT WAY TO HEALTH AND LONGER LIFE

Lester Morrison, M.D.

The famous best-seller that has helped millions gain robust health and increased life span through simple changes in diet, the use of nutritional supplements and weight control. With menus, recipes, life-giving diets, and programs endorsed by distinguished medical authorities. **$1.65**

CARLSON WADE'S HEALTH FOOD RECIPES FOR GOURMET COOKING Carlson Wade

Hundreds of recipes for preparing natural health foods—gourmet style—for healthful eating pleasure. The secret of youthful energy and vitality is in the magical powers of vitamins, minerals, enzymes, protein, and other life-giving elements found in **natural foods.** In this new book, noted nutrition expert Carlson Wade shows you how you can make delicious meals prepared with pure, natural foods; seeds, nuts, berries, whole grains, honey, fruits, fish and more. **$1.65**

INTERNATIONAL VEGETARIAN COOKERY

Sonya Richmond

This book proves that vegetarian cookery, far from being dull and difficult to prepare, can open up completely new and delightful vistas of haute cuisine. Miss Richmond, who has traveled throughout the world, has arranged the book alphabetically according to countries, starting with Austria and going through to the United States. She gives recipes for each country's most characteristic vegetarian dishes and lists that country's outstanding cheeses.

Clothbound: $3.75
Paperbound: $1.75

HEALTH, FITNESS, and MEDICINE BOOKS

QUALITY PAPERBACK BOOKS

Designed to Instruct and Entertain
Each book written by an expert in his field

Aeromodeling, $1.45

The Amateur Psychologist's
    Dictionary, 95¢

Antique Collectors'
    Dictionary, $1.95

The Art of Riding, $1.45

Astrology, 95¢

An Astrology Guide to Your
    Sex Life, 95¢

The Books of Charms and
    Talismans, 95¢

Boy or Girl? Names for Every
    Child, 95¢

Cheiro's Book of Numbers, 95¢

Cheiro's Language of the
    Hand, 95¢

Cheiro's Palmistry for All, 95¢

Cheiro's When You Were Born, 95¢

Collegian's Guide to Part-Time
    Employment, 95¢

The Complete Guide to
    Palmistry, 95¢

Divorce and Annulment in the
    50 States, $1.45

Every Girl's Book of Sex, 95¢

Find Your Job and Land It, 95¢

French: 3100 Steps to Master
    Vocabulary, $1.95

Gift Wrapping, 95¢

Guide to Personality Through
    Your Handwriting, $1.45

Home Brewing Without
    Failures, 95¢

How to Get a Job Overseas, $1.45

How to Win at Gin Rummy, 95¢

Judo and Self-Defense, 95¢

Knots and Splices, 95¢

Mas Oyama's Karate, 95¢

New Traps in the Chess
    Opening, $1.45

1,000 Ideas for English Term
    Papers, $1.45

131 Magic Tricks for Amateurs, 95¢

Practical Guide to Antique
    Collecting, $1.45

Practice for Scholastic Aptitude
    Tests, 95¢

The Production and Staging
    of Plays, 95¢

Profitable Poker, $1.95

Remembering Made Easy, 95¢

Spanish: 3100 Steps to Master
    Vocabulary, $1.95

Successful Winemaking at
    Home, 95¢

Towards Aquarius, $1.45

2,300 Steps to Word Power, $1.45

Upholstery, $1.45

Wake Up and Write, 95¢

Woodturning, 95¢

You Can Find a Fortune, $1.45

Arthritis Can Be Cured, $1.45

Foods Facts and Fallacies, $1.45

Foods for Glamour, $1.65

Get Well Naturally, $1.65

Health Foods and Herbs, 95¢

Healthy Hair, $1.45

Heart Disease and High Blood
    Pressure, $1.45

Herb Growing for Health, $1.65

How to Be Healthy with Natural
    Foods, $1.45

How to Be Healthy with Yoga, 95¢

International Vegetarian
    Cookery, $1.75

Low Blood Sugar and Your
    Health, $1.65

Magic Minerals—Your Key to
    Better Health, $1.95

Muscle Building for Beginners, 95¢

90 Days to a Better Heart, $1.45

The Soybean Cookbook, $1.45

Vitamin E: Your Key to a Healthy
    Heart, $1.65

Weightlifting and Weight
    Training, 95¢

Yoga for Beauty, 95¢